Unstoppable Women

DOES EDUCATION MATTER?

Sarah Wamala Andersson, PhD
Linley Chiwona-Karltun, PhD
Pauline Ocaya, PhD

authorHOUSE®

AuthorHouse™ UK
1663 Liberty Drive
Bloomington, IN 47403 USA
www.authorhouse.co.uk
Phone: 0800.197.4150

Published by AuthorHouse 07/06/2016

ISBN: 978-1-5246-3193-2 (sc)
ISBN: 978-1-5246-3194-9 (hc)
ISBN: 978-1-5246-3195-6 (e)

Print information available on the last page.

Contents

Background

Without question, it is recognized that people of African descent have been very successful when it comes to music, arts, and sports. However, when it comes to higher education, persons of African descent – in particular, women – are under-represented.

Global society has gained high levels of knowledge mainly because of technological advancement which is accessible to a large percentage of the world population. Education levels have increased since the 1970s. For example, Statistics Sweden demonstrates that today 25 percent of the population in Sweden aged twenty-five to sixty-four years has a minimum of college education compared with 10 percent at the beginning of the 1990s.

However, only two percent of people with African backgrounds (one or both parents from Africa) were reported to have enrolled at a university in Sweden. When it comes to PhD studies enrolment, the corresponding figure for people with African background is less than one percent, of which a large proportion are guest students who do not reside permanently in Sweden. Among the university staff, the proportion is low and that group is dominated by guest scientists temporarily living in Sweden.

Why This Book?

Africa has fifty-five countries, with over two thousand languages and a population exceeding one billion people. In spite of the large size and huge variation of flora, sauna and the people that Africa offers, a small proportion of original stories are told by people of African descent.

Sarah Wamala Andersson, Linley Chiwona-Karltun, and Pauline Ocaya are all Karolinska Institutet alumni who graduated with PhDs in medical sciences. They got together and decided to tell the stories about how they attained the highest education levels and the benefits that they have experienced because of that. This book demonstrates unique and powerful stories of three women trailblazers of African descent in Sweden whose lives have been shaped by their higher education and their early lives.

The purpose of this book is to inspire young women and men particularly those who want to live a better and a more meaningful life.

Summary of Stories

The stories in this book are told by three incredible women – Sarah, Linley, and Pauline. All of them have three things in common: they were born and raised in Africa (Malawi or Uganda), they have earned the highest level of education (PhD) in Sweden, and they are unstoppable!

Sarah Wamala Andersson. Sarah was born and raised in a rural village in Uganda by two incredible women – her mother (a teacher) and her grandmother (a self-taught midwife and health worker). In spite of a childhood dominated by many unknowns about her father, worries about school fees, civil wars, and strife, Sarah was the first person ever from her village to graduate with a university degree. Sarah migrated to Sweden at the age of twenty-three, knowing very little about where this path was going to lead her. Along with her, she had a hundred US dollars, a university degree, and a cheap suitcase full of lousy clothes. Fearless of the many challenges that came her way, Sarah determinedly attained her PhD in medical sciences from Karolinska Institutet in 1999 at the age of thirty-two. Sarah was the first-ever person of African descent to be appointed as director general by the Swedish Government in 2008. Parallel to her tenure as director general, Sarah became one of a few professors of African descent at Karolinska Institutet in 2014. Besides Sarah's career journey, her life has been equally taken up with caring for her family, including her daughter with disabilities. Sarah's humble beginnings in Kituntu did not stop her from building a life in Sweden from nothing to a high middle-class level. Yes, Sarah's story confirms that with the right mindset, faith, and determination, high education can be used as a powerful tool towards a better life. Sarah is currently working as an independent international advisor in health systems and leadership development.

Linley Chiwona-Karltun. Born in rural Malawi, Linley was quickly transported into the world of the Western elite at a very early age. Her father, an Oxford graduate, decided very early that he would prepare his daughter to attain higher education. At the age of seven years, Linley was sent to an all-white, Caucasian primary school in Malawi. But her father's political imprisonment when she was thirteen years old nearly brought Linley's education to an end. Undeterred, both father and daughter continued to pursue Linley's higher education. At seventeen, Linley was sent to a boarding school in England. When she was nineteen, Linley went on to the United States to undertake her university education. Her father, knowing well the perils of a young girl, equipped her with an American Express card, telling her, "Any time you have a problem, you can fall back on this card and come back home. Never get yourself into a corner without a way out." Having completed her studies in the United States, Linley went back "home" to Ethiopia in 1987 where her family lived in exile. It was in Ethiopia that she would have her introduction to Sweden, having met a Swedish nutritionist who told her about tuition-free higher education, and in 1988, she migrated to Sweden to continue her pursuit of higher education. In 2001, at the age of thirty-eight, Linley attained her PhD in medical sciences from the Karolinska Institutet. Linley is currently working as a senior scientist at the Swedish University of Agricultural Sciences.

Pauline Ocaya. Pauline was born to a well-educated father who moved from Uganda to work for a Germany construction company in Kenya, and to a mother who was a housewife. Pauline's father migrated to Sweden from war-torn Uganda in the 1990s, and Pauline came later at the age of twelve. Pauline was awarded a PhD in medical sciences from Örebro University in 2007 at the age of twenty-seven. After three years of postdoctoral training at Cornell University, she returned to Sweden in 2011. Barely thirty years old, Pauline was headhunted by three prestigious universities for a research career, and she chose Karolinska Institutet. It was at that time when she decided to embark on studies in medicine. Pauline's story illustrates how one can overcome barriers and shape his or her destiny through determination and the power of higher education. Pauline is currently studying medicine at Umeå University where she lectures in human histology and is the president of the Swedish Medical Students Association in Umeå.

This book provides an overview of the incredible stories of three unstoppable women who decided to seize the moment every time the opportunity for higher education came their way. This book powerfully illustrates what drove these women to attain better lives through higher education, and how they conscientiously overcame their adversities and took decisive actions.

After reading this book, we hope that you will discover the hidden power within you. Regardless of where you are, you will no longer allow circumstances to control your life and hinder you from reaching your full potential. The stories of the three women in this book should motivate, encourage, and affirm that making the choice to study is a meaningful cause. No matter what you choose to do after that, an education can never be stripped away from you. Education will always be beneficial to you at any point in life and in any society.

Sarah Wamala Andersson, PhD

No Excuses for Humble Beginnings in Africa

I believe that with the right mindset and the burning desire to become better and greater every day, high education can enable you to achieve your goals and live a better life.

Acknowledgements

To my wonderful family: my fabulous daughter Erina for being a great inspiration for me to use the hidden power within me and tell my story; my incredible daughter Nellie for asking me intelligent questions about my life; and my loving husband, Per, for listening to my story several times over the years, for your brilliant feedback and wisdom, and for supporting me to finally tell my story.

To my lovely sisters Edith and Ritah for filling in the missing gaps and for the laughter we have shared over the years about my story.

To my dearest friends and colleagues, Matt for reading my story and giving me your invaluable and intelligent feedback and Ingrid for your wise insights on various aspects. To my dear friend Angelica for your excellent feedback.

To my dear relatives, Ida for your wise feedback, and Stina for encouraging me to tell my story (even if it has taken time).

I would like to acknowledge all the incredible people, wherever you are, for being part of my experiences and my story.

My deep gratitude to the grace of higher powers for guidance, strength, and wisdom to tell my story based on incredible experiences.

Early Life

I was born in Kituntu village, 60 kilometres south of Kampala, the capital city of Uganda. My first given name was "Night", meaning a child born at night. I grew up on a farm with my mother, Justine Namuli, and my grandmother, Robinah Kamasazi, and I was the eldest of seven siblings. My grandmother was short, muscular, light skinned, short haired, kind, intuitive, structured, principled, and hard to mess with. My mother was tall, light skinned, slim, long haired, strikingly beautiful, spontaneous, warm but strict though she often wore a smile.

My grandmother was a Tutsi who migrated from Rwanda to Uganda, fleeing the ethnic tensions. She fled with her parents, her husband and children. Her father died on the way and her husband died shortly after arrival in Uganda. She gave birth to eleven children, of these only two survived (my mother and my uncle). We were referred to as *banyolo*, meaning "outsiders" or "immigrants," who were regarded as second-class citizens. Regardless of the new generation in Uganda, we were still regarded as *banyolo*. We looked different from most typical Ugandans: taller, slender and lighter skinned. This seemed to cause envy, especially among women and girls. My grandmother was committed to compensating for the negative consequences of us being *banyolo*. She worked hard and carried out extensive community work, including providing and advising about health, hygiene, sanitation, food, water, housing, and roads. My grandmother made sure that her children (my mother and my uncle) acquired education. In fact, my mother had the highest education of all women in Kituntu. My uncle was also a teacher at another school several kilometres away. He used his bike as transport to and from the school.

I had a lot of fun during my childhood. I particularly enjoyed watching and learning from my mother and grandmother contributing to the community development of Kituntu in different ways. My mother helped many children to acquire education. My grandmother was a self-taught but illiterate health and community worker. She helped

7

many women to safely deliver their babies, and not a single baby died in her hands. She gave health advice to women in pre- and postnatal periods, including basic hygiene and what/how to feed themselves and their babies. She delivered all her grandchildren and my mother never gave birth in a hospital. I remember my youngest brother, Gift, was born premature, at twenty-eight weeks, weighing about 800 grams. My mother had a complicated delivery which went on for three days. My grandmother attended my mother, and she constructed an incubator for Gift and cared for him. No trained health personnel attended him, and they never needed to go to the hospital. Gift is a hardworking and smart young man who is now twenty-nine years old, and he has been living and working in South Africa for the last six years.

My grandmother had an extraordinary knowledge of the jungle and its vast plants that could cure or prevent several illnesses. Additionally, she applied basic hygiene both at home and in her community work. I don't remember that we needed to visit hospitals to get treatment. There were many incidences when we contracted with malaria and many other tropical diseases, and she cured them instantly.

My grandmother also had excellent farming knowledge, and she successfully grew different types of food crops and cash crops on the farm and raised different types of farm animals. She hired men who were looking for jobs to work on the farm. The farm not only sustained the family and relatives but also sustained other families in Kituntu. She had knowledge about the nutrition advantages and disadvantages of different types of food.

We were not allowed to drink water that had not been boiled. Boiled water was always available in a big pot, *'ensuwa'* (which functioned as a refrigerator) in our sitting room. It tasted very good (I still remember the taste).

We lived in a large, brick house, which my grandmother built herself with some help from the men she hired to work on the farm. She also constructed houses for different purposes on the farm, for example, for keeping the crop harvest and seeds and for the farm animals.

My grandmother was concerned about safe water, sanitation, hygiene, nutrition, housing, and roads. She was good at motivating and organizing men and boys in Kituntu to assist. She led and instructed them to clean water wells, clear roads, and assist in big crop harvests.

My grandmother was highly respected for her broad wisdom and generosity, which made her an informal village leader and a respected health community worker. That way, we gained respect and suffered lesser negative consequences of being *banyolo*.

Starting School

I started my first class at Masiko Primary School at the age of five. Because my mother was a teacher at Masiko, my siblings and I had the opportunity to start school early. We felt blessed to have the opportunity to go to school. Many other children, particularly girls, in Kituntu could not go to school because they lacked the money to pay school fees or the parents didn't believe in educating girls. I remember the long and exciting walk of 5 kilometres (one way), that we used to take every day to school. In spite of walking a long distance barefoot on a dusty/ muddy road, we used to play a lot. Particularly on the way back from school, we were engaged in finding short cuts and picking fruits and berries which made the walking distance shorter and exciting. During the rainy season, it was very slippery and muddy, and we would come to school with very dirty feet. This was not strange in any way, as many children, particularly in the first classes, did not have shoes, and in fact, I don't recall that any child in my first two classes had shoes. My mother bought me the first pair of leather shoes when I was seven years old. The traces of walking a long distance without shoes can be traced on my toenails, some of which are damaged, as they were crushed by the stones. I think this is why I love shoes of different types.

Because my mother was a respected teacher, we experienced a special treatment at school, but the expectations of us were very high. We were expected to set a good example. We looked different from the rest. My nickname in Masiko Primary School was "Bright" (meaning "intelligent" or "light skinned"). Some of my friends still call me "Bright." I showed a high academic talent at an early age. I remember earning gifts for the best handwriting as early as five years old.

Daily Activities in Kituntu

Because I was the eldest of my seven siblings, I was expected to take the biggest responsibility for household chores and to lead my siblings. The household chores included helping on the farm with the cultivation of food and cash crops and taking care of the animals (cattle, goats, sheep, chicken, rabbits, etc.), collecting water from a well in the forest (1.5 kilometres from our house), collecting firewood from the forest (learnt to fight with snakes and learnt behaviours of a lion family which lived permanently in the bushes), making baskets, constructing our beds, cleaning, preparing and cooking food, etc. We were busy most of the time, but playing at the same time which was fun. For some reasons, my siblings would often avoid work. I learned quickly to lead them as a team and motivate them to help out with the household chores.

Our family's income came from selling coffee, cotton, poultry, cattle, and a variety of food crops, and my mother's salary from teaching. My mother used to trade food to the school against paying school fees for us and for other children who my mother helped to acquire school education. My grandmother was never paid cash for her public health services.

I spent a lot of time with my grandmother and learnt many things from her. My grandmother taught me how to handle finances and many other spheres of life. I also believe that she inspired me to acquire training in public health sciences.

I particularly remember that my grandmother used to say: *"It is not about how much money you have, but it is all about how well you use it."* I still apply this learning in my daily life and I appreciate this.

Our society perceived every child as an investment for the whole community. We were free to play in other homes, and adults cared for all children, not only their own. I enjoyed picking fruits, and I especially enjoyed climbing tall trees to pick mangoes, avocado, jackfruits, etc. Unlike my siblings, who used to eat at neighbours' houses, I did not want to eat meals outside our household. This is because my mother and my grandmother had a very high standard of hygiene which I didn't perceive to be followed in other households. Sometimes neighbours would report me to my grandmother for being impolite and ungrateful.

The weekends in Kituntu were exciting and lively. Saturday was a day for selling and buying different sorts of things and meeting friends and relatives. There was a market in Kituntu trading centre where people gathered, coming from villages near and far to either buy or sell various commodities. We used to help my mother and my grandmother sell various kinds of things in the market. Local musicians played music. It was also a meeting place for many people and quite fun.

Sunday was a day to praise God. Everyone wore his or her best clothes and had the most delicious food after the church together with visitors (we always had visitors on Sundays). The most delicious food for us was often '*matooke*' (green bananas) steamed in banana leaves with chicken stew or groundnuts sauce, also steamed in banana leaves and several different kinds of vegetables on the side. I miss this food!

My mother was a Lutheran Protestant, but my grandmother was not sure about Christianity, as she believed that there were some African gods who protected us, made the sun shine, women fertile and plants grow. My mother was active in church, which was at Masiko School where she was a teacher, and she used to take us all to the church, and encouraged us to sing in the church. We enjoyed singing in the church, and we practiced at home frequently. It was enjoyable. My grandmother wondered how people responded to our singing, and she wanted to hear us singing in the church. She decided to start attending church on Sundays. The pastor talked with her about Christianity, and she decided that since it was not harmful to her and her family, she would consider becoming a Christian. I still remember the day when my grandmother got baptized. It was a great moment for us, and this is when she acquired her English name, Robinah. It is not known why they picked Robinah, but I remember that she felt ok with her new English name. Nevertheless, she continued to believe in the African gods.

My mother and grandmother kept on telling us that the worst thing that could happen to a young girl was to "play with boys" and become pregnant. They were very keen on seeing to it that boys would not get any closer to us. It was education and only education that mattered, nothing else. Education became almost like a doctrine for us. I was constantly told, "If you want to eat bread, you have to get an education, but if you want to eat bread with butter, you have to attain the highest education." This message was very clear to us. We had no possibility to bake bread. We had to buy bread from the trading centre, and it was expensive. Therefore, we only had bread on very special occasions.

Continuing School and Starting Secondary School

Masiko Primary School had seven classes through the last primary class (class seven), after which students would study further at secondary school level. I made top grades all the way, and I never repeated any class. I passed the primary-graduation examination with distinctions. I was ready to study further in secondary school. However, my family lacked the money to pay for my secondary school. There were no secondary schools close to Kituntu. It had to be a boarding school, which required students to be full-time residents in school. These schools were very expensive for my family's financial standing. Therefore, I had to repeat class seven three times while my grandmother and mother were gathering money to send me to secondary school. I was almost frustrated, having to repeat the same class after making high grades every year. On the hand, my mother and grandmother felt that this was a safe way for me to be in school until they could raise money for my secondary school fees. Many girls in Kituntu who did not go to school got married as young as thirteen years old.

My mother started to look for other higher-paying jobs than teaching. She finally got a new job as a local government clerk in Ggoli about 30 kilometres away from Kituntu. She wanted to raise the money to get me to the secondary school. This is the first time my mother lived outside Kituntu, and it was a great change for the whole family, especially my grandmother. My mother took my younger sister Betty (who died at the age of twenty) and me to join her in Ggoli. My younger siblings stayed in Kituntu with my grandmother. We used to go back to Kituntu on the weekends and we used to take with us food that would last the whole week. That way, my mother did not need to worry about food expenses. My mother took me to a nearby school, Ggoli Primary School (a Catholic school), to attend class seven (repeating the third time). I was happier to repeat class seven in another school than at Masiko.

My search for a higher meaning of life started when I was at Ggoli. Because I was well-behaved and was the best in my class, I was liked by teachers, especially the nuns. I participated in the church activities, and I admired the nuns, their uniforms, and their dedication to God. The nuns convinced me that I would be a great nun if I decided to go to a nuns' school and study to become one. This would not require me to pay any school fees, which was enticing to me. I told my mother and grandmother about my plans. I will never forget the strong negative reaction that I received from both of them. They made it vividly clear to me that there was no way they would let me become a nun. I had to drop the whole idea. I got to understand later that their burning issue was about me staying unmarried and having no children.

I earned top grades from Ggoli, and I was the best in the whole district. This time my mother had saved some money from her new job, which was complemented with selling some animals and crops from the farm in Kituntu. They decided to send me to the boarding school, Ndejje Secondary School, 150 kilometres away from Kituntu. Ndejje was a mixed school of both girl and boy students. I had excellent grades, and it was not a problem to get enrolled in better secondary schools than Ndejje, and Ndejje was relatively less expensive than other schools in the city.

When I started at Ndejje, I only had the basic major requirements for school, and I lacked most of the necessities. We wore school uniforms all the time during weekdays. The motto of Ndejje was "No pain, no gain," and this was sown on our uniforms. I believed in this motto, that with hard work (even if it sometimes came with some pain) in school, I could realise the gains later (I have kept a piece of the rug that was sown on my uniform until today). This belief has motivated me over the years.

(Photo of the Ndejje secondary school badge with the motto)

In Ndejje, some students used to call me *longido*, meaning a "tall person" in a negative way, especially for girls, as they were generally shorter and not expected to be taller than boys. I could hear from a distance when some students used to laugh and whisper that *Longido* is coming. I remember that I sometimes walked with my legs bent to stand at the shorter height of other girls.

My first thirteen years had been protected from issues and worries of relative poverty. It was at the Ndejje that it occurred to me that I came from a poor family as compared to other students. I had not experienced this earlier in my life. This was when my interest in socio-economic issues started. In Kituntu, we had everything we needed. We lived in a large house, and we had almost everything we needed from the farm, including candies (sugar cane) and plenty of food, and we had a high status because of what my mother and grandmother offered to the Kituntu inhabitants. We had been among the top families who were better off, but in Ndejje, it was the opposite.

Many students were boasting about their rich and great fathers. Not having a father hadn't mattered for me in Kituntu but it mattered in Ndejje. I had to make up stories about my father, which made feel bad. I felt a bit uncomfortable to see that other students had a lot of materialistic stuff which I did not have. Most of them came from richer families in Kampala and other bigger cities. Only a few students came from rural villages as I did. However, I had a competitive advantage of a higher intellectual capacity than other students. Other students were constantly asking for my notes and my guidance in studies, particularly in mathematics and sciences. I quickly identified a "source of income". I started to exchange my study-help services for stuff from richer students that I lacked. There was no problem for these rich students, as it was easy to ask their families for new stuff as long as they went home with good grades. Because of my intellectual talents, high level of discipline, and participation in sports and other associations, I quickly gained high status at Ndejje. I received prizes and recognition for my school performance and as a role model for many other students. Already in the second grade, I was elected to lead various clubs at school. I later got elected as the head girl, leading all girl students (about two hundred girls).

At that time (and even still today), the school education was organized as follows: primary school (seven years), secondary school (four years), higher secondary school (three years), and university (minimum three years). At the end of each of these levels, students' knowledge was tested using similar standardized examinations at a national level. These exams started at primary school grade 7. The examinations were coordinated and administered by the Ministry of Education and were similar for every school in the whole country. Additionally, there were class exams for every level. Students who failed to pass the examinations were required to repeat the class until they passed in order to move on to the next level.

During my second grade in secondary school, my mother and grandmother failed to raise my school fees. They sadly told me that I could not continue school. I remember those long two weeks in Kituntu when my schoolmates had started school, but I could not be there because of lack of school fees. It was a difficult time, full of tears and worries. I knew that education was a master key to my future, only seeing this vanishing away in front of my eyes. I feared that if I missed the whole term, I could never make it back to school, and I would somehow be forced to get married to an older village man as many of the girls did. This was the worst scenario that could happen to me.

I was deeply worried about taking a similar path as others girls in Kituntu. A path they were expected to take – low/no education, getting married as a child, carrying out hard work everyday and giving birth to a dozen children.

I was fiercely determined to go back to school, no matter what. I thought that if I could just tell the school management that my family had failed to raise my school fees, just maybe there could be some solution. My grandmother managed to get me some money, just enough for my bus trip to Ndejje and for some pocket money. I was terrified, and I avoided the headmaster's office during the first days, but I had to face my fear.

At one of the physics lessons, I told my physics teacher about my school fees problem. I was the best physics student, and the teacher got very concerned. The next day, the teacher advised me to apply for a scholarship for orphans. I fulfilled the criteria of being supported as an orphan, as I was told that my father had died when I was a baby. I completed the forms, and the next step was to take them to my home district for approval. I got the permission to travel to Kampala on the school truck with no cost. I used the pocket money that my grandmother had given me to buy a bus ticket from Kampala to Mpigi (my home district offices), about 40 kilometres from Kampala. I recall the long hours and the hunger and thirst I felt while waiting outside the district commissioner's office in Mpigi. I was fourteen years old and shy. I watched many people walking in and out of the commissioner's office (mostly men). I was afraid to open my mouth to tell anyone what I needed. I had learnt that children were not expected to talk with adults if the adults did not initiate the talking. I realized that time was going by, and I had to be on time in Kampala to get to the school truck back to Ndejje, with a commissioner's stamp on my application. I finally gathered the guts and asked for help from a woman (seemed to be an administrator). I told the woman why I was there, and the woman was touched by my story. She took me directly to the commissioner's office. Finally, I had a stamp on my application forms to take back to Ndejje. I was extremely happy and grateful! I made it to the school truck in time, and the next morning I delivered the stamped forms. I received a letter from the headmaster that I was offered an orphanage scholarship. I felt relieved and grateful. My anxiety about school fees was now solved, as this scholarship would cover all my school fees for the entire secondary and high-level secondary school as long as I stayed in the same school, Ndejje. My burning desire and determination to pursue education forced me to find soultions about school fees during a situation where I had nothing.

My remaining problem was to raise money for my school necessities, pocket money, and transport to and from school. I had to find a solution, so I asked my grandmother if I could use part of the farm to grow crops for sale. My grandmother gave me the best cultivatable piece of land. I started to raise money through farming and selling cash crops. I was successful at yielding profitable harvests. I also started to trade in various ways in Kituntu and the nearby villages. For example, I started to buy raw, unprocessed groundnuts and put my siblings at work getting them ready for sale in the trading centre. I also "employed" my cousins and siblings to assist me on the farm to grow crops which I later sold to the market and earned money. With these financial ventures, in addition to my orphanage scholarship, I could independently sustain my school education without worrying my family.

At the secondary school level national exams, I and a male student were the best students in the whole district, and Ndejje was highly recognized for this achievement. I remember the school party that was thrown in celebration, and I can never forget the present that I received from the school, a nice, purple dress which I used to wear on special occasions. I kept it well many years.

Teenage and Searching for the Meaning of Life

My teenage period was preoccupied with education, hunting for school fees, worries about war and conflicts, asking questions about my father, and finding the meaning of life.

In spite of the several questions that I posed about my father, my mother and grandmother refused to answer these questions. All these things were kept as a big secret. They told me that my father had died when I was a baby (I did not believe this). I never saw my father, and until today I know anything about him. I never saw any photo of him. I kept on imagining what he looked like, where he came from, how his family was, and if he cared about me. I wondered when he would finally show up. I was most of the time angry about my father, and I could not understand why he did not take any responsibility. I felt ashamed at school for not knowing anything about my father.

My search for a higher meaning of life continued after Ggoli. At the age of fourteen, I became friends with a girl by the name of Victoria, who was at higher secondary school level in Ndejje. Victoria came from a Seventh - Day Adventist family, and she was very committed to Adventism. I got curious about this religion, and I borrowed many books from Victoria to read about Seventh-Day Adventism (SDA). I read many books on SDA, and I was inspired. I think I was looking for something to hold on to in order to be able to carry myself through the tough life experiences and to minimize risks that were facing many young people by then. I was totally sold on the SDA spiritual beliefs. I realized that SDA did more good than harm, and it would protect me from many risks that included keeping my body pure from the use of alcohol, drugs, tobacco, and, most importantly, not to indulge in premarital sexual relationships and end up becoming pregnant. I had witnessed many girls destroying their future by becoming pregnant at an early age.

When I returned to Kítuntu for school holidays, I broke the news to my family that I had converted from Lutheran Christianity to SDA. It was not the belief itself that was controversial, but it was the whole thing about changing routines at home. My family used to go to church on Sundays, yet SDAs praise God on the Sabbath day, Saturday. Saturday was a day for many happenings in Kituntu – now it would be a holy day, where buying and selling activities were not allowed. I was so committed to the SDA that I also influenced my siblings, and they joined me in prayers on Saturdays. In fact, I am not sure that they believed in the SDA. I think that they enjoyed the idea of changing the previously busy Saturday into a calm prayer day with less to do. My mother and grandmother kept a low profile, possibly because they had previously refused to let me become a nun or they understood that SDA was doing more good and it would keep me away from the risks they were afraid for.

Experiences and Survival from War and Conflicts

Unlike many of my friends who changed to other schools after secondary school, I could not change to another school, as I would lose my scholarship which covered my school fees. I had to return to Ndejje even when there was a high risk of war and conflicts in that region. I was focused on studying further at higher secondary school (HSc).

At HSc level, students were required to choose their majors and specialize in three subjects. My mother and grandmother were expecting me to become a physician, and it was no problem, as I had top grades in sciences and mathematics. Additionally, I had a vision to contribute to making peoples lives better.

I was sixteen years old when I asked my mother to go for a study visit to a public hospital, (which would be my potential workplace). I was fascinated about this big hospital, which was relatively new. I discovered that patients were lying on the floor waiting in the corridors. Nurses and doctors did not seem to be present to attend to them. I asked what was going on, and I learnt that the doctors and nurses were not paid enough, and they needed to work somewhere else to get extra income to be able to run their household economies. I realized that the biggest problem was poverty, and I wanted to attain an education that would contribute to increasing wealth, reducing poverty and make people's lives better. I decided to major in mathematics and economics at HSc. My mother and my grandmother were not so happy about this, but they could not stop me.

My last two high school years at Ndejje, 1983 to 1986, were mainly dominated by the civil wars which were associated with worries of rape, torture, and killings. We often heard the screaming at night from the camps near our school where displaced people were forced to stay. Girls and women were raped in the night by soldiers. Boys and men were tortured or forced to torture others, and those who were physically strong were forced to join the army. Many people were forced out of their villages and brought to the refuge camps close to our school. The camps were overcrowded, and we witnessed daily through our school fence how people were struggling to get water and food. People lacked latrines, and the hygiene was very unhealthy. I can still smell the odour from the camps. Even during daylight, we could sometimes witness torture. Young men who refused to join the army or who were suspected of supporting rival forces were burned alive. They were forced to carry burning plastic gallons on their heads until they dropped dead with terrible pain.

We, school students were treated as hostages, to prevent the rebel soldiers from being bombed by the rivals. It was understood that there was an agreement between the school management and the rebel soldiers not to harm the students. The soldiers built their military camps close to the boundary of our school. Although they were not "officially" allowed to walk freely in the school dormitories, they came to the dormitories at night looking for girls to rape. In my capacity as a head girl, I raised this problem with the school management, but I received the response that the girls were just scared and overreacting. Soldiers were not allowed to walk in the students' dormitories at any time. I can imagine that the school management had a lot of pressure from both sides. My friends and I were forced to find our own protective strategies. Soldiers had both a persuasive and a forceful tactic. Some soldiers offered students tinned food, biscuits, or money in exchange for sexual exploitation or joining the army. My strategy together with my close friends was to make ourselves so undesirable and unattractive that the soldiers would not even look at us. With the knowledge I learned from my grandmother about plants and weeds, I found plants in the school gardens that we could smear on our bodies which produced a terrible odour from a long distance. This was not desirable.

My friends and I spent the daytime looking for hiding places, which were kept intact and not to be known by any other students. The two best hiding places were the rooftop of our dormitories, which was directly open to the sky and difficult to get to (I appreciated my climbing skills that I had acquired from climbing mango trees in Kituntu). Another one was the stinking sewage trunk hole which had a heavy cement lid. No one would be expected to spend the whole night in these places. We hid in different places every night just after the lights were put out at 22.00 hours. I remember the scary sound of soldiers' boots on the top of the stinking sewage trunk where I was squatting. In the morning, it was difficult to stand up after spending the night squatting in the sewage trunk.

On the rooftop, we used dark blankets, not to be easily seen – here we could hide about ten of us. We could see the soldiers from a distance getting in through the gate to our dormitory. Our hearts were pounding heavily, and we were terribly afraid that they would hear us. The strategy was to "play dead", no sound, and no movement. We studied cautiously their behaviours, including when and how they would get into our dormitories, and how they persuaded some girls to have sexual relationships with them. The school and the lessons were run as "normal": everyone pretended that all was normal. Our protective strategies together with protection from higher powers made it possible for us to escape sexual exploitation and rape, and I am very grateful.

The war got so intense that the headmaster was advised to get the students out of the school campus. The school headmaster ordered us to leave the school immediately and carry pocket money, a school identity card, and a few of our most important belongings. We had to walk several kilometres to search for the next possible safe place. I remember how hard it was to choose which books to carry, as many of them were heavy, yet I needed them in order to be able to pass the final exams to the university. There were only two months left till final exams to qualify for university intake. We walked several miles, and the first safe place we were offered was a primary school several miles from Ndejje. We slept on the dusty floor in classrooms and we were happy that it was relatively safe. The school management took a great responsibility and had packed food and water on the school truck which drove slowly along with us as we were walking. The rebel soldiers also took responsibility to guard and keep the students and teachers safe from other bombings. As the head girl, I was expected to lead students to follow the instructions given by the school management. Thus, the escape felt somewhat safe, although cumbersome, tiresome, and psychologically exhausting.

After a couple of days, it was safer to proceed to Kampala. The school management organized buses to transport students and teachers to Kampala, where it was easier to get students closer to their families. We were all dropped off in Kampala. I had no relatives there. Fortunately, I had some pocket money to buy a bus ticket to my family in Kituntu. My family was very happy to see me again after a long time in Ndejje. I only stayed a few days as I had to get back to Kampala to get prepared for the final exams to get to the university.

Another challenge happened on my way to Kampala. I took a *'matatu'* (small minibus used for public transport) from Kituntu together with eight other passengers. I knew most of them. As we were getting closer to Kampala, the matatu collided with another vehicle crossing from another road. It was early morning, and I was sleepy – only to be woken up by the loud traffic collision. At first, I thought it was a dream. The matatu was pushed across the road and turned upside down. It was all chaos and critical. One woman that I knew from Kituntu was cut heavily in the stomach and died instantly. Two others died in the hospital, and others had serious injuries. I had a bad headache, and my right-hand fingers were injured. I stayed at the hospital for one day. It was only two weeks left till final national exams prior to the university. My thumb and the next two fingers on my right hand were injured so badly that I could not write with my right hand. Thus, I had to exercise writing with the left hand. Additionally, I was looking for accommodation and food. I contacted my SDA friend Victoria for help. She was studying pharmacy at college, and she was staying in a hostel in Kampala. She kindly let me share her room in her hostel while looking for accommodation. It was not allowed to have other people staying in the hostel. I kept on staying with friends in turns. The Ndejje school management collaborated with another secondary school in Kampala to access their lecture rooms for limited teaching. We spent most of the time in a public library which turned out to be a great meeting place with other students who were preparing for the exams. Just as I practiced in Ndejje, I helped other students in maths and sciences, and they, in turn, gave me food and other things that I needed.

It is no wonder that experiences during my school years at Ndejje (between the ages of thirteen and nineteen years) shaped most of my strong character. A large part of my life at that time was filled with fear and anxiety, constant worries about not being able to secure school fees for my education and keeping my self safe from the war conflicts in the region. I am grateful for my faith in higher powers, which was a powerful protecting and comforting factor.

Getting Enrolled at Makerere University

Finally, the final exams were done. The school vacation of several months started. I had to find a job while anxiously waiting for the results from the Ministry of Education. I was blessed to get a job as a shop assistant and to help with bookkeeping in a store in Kampala where they were selling spare parts for Japanese cars. I quickly learned about the spare parts business and made some good money. However, I also witnessed the patriarchal practices, most of which I didn't like at all. I was the only girl working there; all others were older men with no or low education. I was regarded as a "cocky", as I refused to indulge myself in practices that would compromise my faith in higher powers and distract me from achieving my goals. I was street smart and focused on getting to the university. I used the money I earned to buy things that I thought would need at the university and to help my family in Kituntu.

Finally, the results were nailed on the notice board in the main administration building at Makerere University. I had to read my name several times. I could not believe that I was one of those who had made top grades to get enrolled at the university. At that time, Makerere was the only university in the whole of Uganda, and had a high international reputation. Thus, the required grades for enrolment were at a very high level. In spite of the fact that I suffered the civil war at Ndejje, had interruptions in my studies, had a car accident, moved from place to place, and had no relatives in Kampala, I made it to the only university in Uganda. I still remember that feeling, with my heart pumping hard, with the understanding that I was now joining the educated elites' club. We were three of us from Ndejje high school (myself being the only girl) who made it to the university that year.

Getting enrolled to Makerere and being allocated a student room felt incredibly wonderful. Finally, I had my "own home". I felt a lot of freedom, peace, happiness, gratitude and motivation. At that time, university students were offered free accommodation and free meals at Makerere. I was one of the twenty students (five girls) at the university who had qualified to study economics.

At Makerere University, I was called *muzungu,* which means "a white person." In fact, many girls at the university were envious of my height and my light-skinned colour. All these surprised me. Light-skinned girls at the university were regarded as being more beautiful, nicer, more intelligent, and richer than dark-skinned girls. In fact, some girls spent a lot of money buying skin bleaching creams to become lighter skinned. Thus, some girls thought that I could not be so light-skinned unless I used skin breaching creams or was a "half *muzungu*". I found these stories very fascinating as I didn't even know that such skin breaching creams existed, and even so, I could not afford them or want to use them. My friends used to tease me that my father could have been a *muzungu*, yet I had no idea who my father was.

My role as the eldest sibling became stronger. I was expected to mentor and support my siblings in different ways (including paying their school fees). They all depended on me. I used to work hard during weekends and vacations to be able to raise money for my daily living and to take care of my family in Kituntu. During my second year in 1988, my dear grandmother died suddenly (seemed to be a heart attack). This was a big tragedy for me, my family, and Kituntu. My grandmother was the master planner of great things, and many people depended on her. I used to seek advice from her in many aspects of life. I felt empty!

Although I was involved in various activities at the university, my number one priority was to earn top grades. We had an association of university Seventh-Day Adventists which I enjoyed very much and which helped me to keep on my spiritual track. There were several challenges at the university, especially for girls. I spent a lot of time in the library where I could borrow textbooks instead of buying them.

After all the exams and after being awarded our grades, we had to wait several months for the formal graduation ceremony. This was a great celebration for all families and others. I was not there. I had just moved to Sweden. I felt very sad at missing my graduation ceremony. I denied my mother the honour to march with me in my graduation gown and to have a big party to celebrate having become one of the educated elites.

Having to Get Married, Regardless of Academic Successes

In rural Africa, over 50 percent of girls get married when they are still children (below eighteen years of age). Interestingly, even when girls had acquired a high education, they were still pressured to get married. The society perceived women, even when they were highly educated and had high-paying jobs, as failures when they were not married. These expectations caused (still do) a lot of stress among many female students at the university beyond their study demands and other challenges.

During the final year at the university, some students started planning for further education in Europe, North America, or Australia. Most of them had relatives abroad or had powerful family networks in Uganda which enabled them to access international scholarships. It was more about which family and relatives you had than about performance per se in order to get access to international scholarships. I had no such networks, and it was hard to access any international scholarship. Girls who had the opportunity to get a scholarship happily escaped the pressure of marriage plans.

During my final year at Makerere University, I was approached by an older woman at the SDA church (we call her Betha). Betha told me how she was impressed about my good behaviours, being pretty, and being a university student. Betha told me that she had a brother who lived and worked in Sweden and he was looking for a young, well-educated young woman with my qualities to marry.

The final year was very stressful for several female students at the university as they were expected to have plans to get married on top of passing exams and getting a well-paying job. My mother was more concerned about me earning a high-class university degree and getting a well-paying job. However, like many other families, she had pressure from others.

Finally, I agreed to meet Betha's brother (I call him Dande). I met Dande in Kampala while he was on holidays. Dande responded to Betha that he had met his dream woman to marry. The university girls were generally very attractive for marriage to many men, although they were not expected to practice their intellectual independency. Dande was very excited and wanted me to join him as soon as possible. I was determined to pursue my utmost goal – to attain my university degree – and nothing would stop me. Dande demonstrated everything about himself and his life in Sweden to look more impressive and attractive than it really was.

When I met Dande the second time, he told me that he needed to work on my visa requirements to travel to Sweden and that we needed to go together to the city council. Dande had already organized a form for me to sign. Dande being an older man and a Seventh Day Adventist,

I thought I could trust him. After signing the form, Dande told me that we were now legally married and that I had just signed a marriage certificate. I could not believe it. I felt robbed of my freedom to make my own independent decision. Dande did not respect several other traditional routines towards marriage. My grandmother would never have accepted that, but she was gone!

This was the time when HIV/AIDS had started to kill off many people (especially the youths), and it was a difficult time. Just like several other young women, I was worried that I had limited chances of having a safe sexual relationship in a society where men freely had multiple relationships. Additionally, I discovered that the job which was available for me at one of the banks had workplace politics that were not compatible with my values. Regardless of their performance level, young women were (secretly) expected to have sexual relationships with male managers in order to get a job, keep a job, or get a promotion. Generally, I was not at peace with many things, particularly, how women were expected to be and to behave in society. I had many incidences from an early age when I had to constantly find strategies and sometimes fight to protect myself from being sexually exploited by different boys and men. Many other things were going on including a political instability. I hated all these. All these things in addition to my passion for further education created a discontent and a burning desire for me to leave.

My grandmother was not alive, and I badly needed her to advise me. I had faith in higher powers, and I prayed many times for guidance. Finally, I made a decision based on my brain rather than my heart. I was convinced that my future would take a different trajectory if I migrated to Europe. I had the option to join Dande as his wife in Sweden, although I was scared of him. I did not know Dande well, and I didn't know much about Sweden, besides a few facts based on my geography lessons. At the same time, I felt grateful to have this option, so I made a decision to grab the opportunity. I remember talking with my young sister Ritah, crying and devastated, but determined to join Dande and do the best as a wife, and to find better opportunities in Europe. I knew my grandmother would advise me to do that.

My Journey to Sweden

It was August when I came to Sweden. I had a cheap suitcase full of lousy clothes and a hundred US dollars. On my way from the airport, I was fascinated about the perfect, wide roads; beautiful rocks; thick and green forests; and dried woods. The dried woods made me wonder why no one was collecting them. Recalling how we used to struggle to find firewoods to take home for cooking. I just wanted to haul away these woods to send to the girls and women in Kituntu.

Life with Dande was far different from what I had anticipated. After my three months' visitors' visa expired, Dande refused to process residence and work permits for me to stay in Sweden. I could not understand what was going on. It appeared that Dande had brought several young women from Uganda to Sweden and threw them out after their tourist visas had expired. These are examples of the very patriarchal practices that I was running away from Uganda, only to catch me up in a highly democratic country. I was legally married to Dande. I knew that I needed to get a divorce from Dande to be able to move freely forward. Dande did not want to divorce.

I am very grateful to Sweden and its policies of supporting women, particularly when they get into troubles related to patriarchal practices.

It all started with me being the first girl ever from Kituntu, against all odds, making it to the only university and attaining a university degree. And it is because of my university education, good qualities, and faith in higher powers that Dande wanted to marry me without even asking for my permission. I believe that the higher powers used Dande as a vessel for me to migrate to Sweden and to be able to live a better life and make other people's lives better. I cannot begin to speculate on how my life would be if I stayed in Uganda. Many of my friends, beautiful and talented, died of HIV/AIDS in their early twenties.

I cherish learning lessons from all the challenges that I have experienced. In fact, getting through all those challenges, in addition to my high education and faith, has built my strong character, to become that unstoppable woman.

Creating a New Life in the New Country

I learnt that there were no different categories of black people in relation to treatment as it was in Uganda. I was not regarded as a *'muzungu'* as it was in Uganda. I was regarded as any other black person. Surprisingly, it appeared that being a black person was not a good thing. Although I had experienced being an outsider in Uganda, the experiences of being an outsider in Sweden felt different and new. At the same time, I met many kind and helpful people who made things easier for me in a difficult time.

I was determined to be financially independent and to quickly get integrated into the Swedish society. I decided to put my university degree aside and find a paying job. I was reading many adverts in the newspaper. I applied for several unskilled jobs, and finally, I was hired as a cleaner at a post office. Cleaning at the post office was painful after attaining a unique university degree from Makerere University and being one of the few educated elites. On the other hand, this forced me to impatiently find my way into the Swedish academic arena. At the post office, none of the colleagues believed that I had attained a university degree. Others who knew were mocking me for working as a cleaner after attaining a university degree. I knew what I was doing and I was focused. Yet all these things created a discontent and a burning desire to do whatever it took to study further and get a job that matched my educational attainment.

I was working during the day and attending evening classes in Swedish language, accounting, and computer sciences. I had an ambitious target – to attain a PhD by the age of thirty (I came to Sweden at the age of twenty-three). Given my prevailing circumstances, this dream was far from being realistic. I was thrilled and grateful that I could pursue higher education in Sweden without experiencing the stresses of looking for school fees as I did in Uganda. After several visits to the Agency of Employment Services, I finally succeeded to enrol in a one-year training programme which ended with a trainee programme. Thanks to a woman officer at the agency who was understanding and provided me this opportunity. This was about one year since I had started to work at the post office.

I am still grateful for my job as a cleaner. I learnt a lot from my supervisor - a Finnish woman, about cleaning and what detergents to use in different ways. I quickly learned about how workplaces in Sweden function, and I learned to drink Swedish coffee. I found out that coffee drinking is an important part of workplace politics in Sweden. I understood that failing to interact in the coffee breaks would negatively affect your career development. Interestingly, I heard many things and secrets, as they thought that I did not understand much Swedish. I learned to clean properly, which I find useful in my daily life. It is at the post office where I participated in the first training about legal aspects of work and the role of labour unions. My cleaning job gave me the financial possibility to plan, manage my bills and support my family in Uganda. More importantly, I became independent, successfully divorced from Dande, and started building up my life. While some were buying expensive leather sofa sets on credit, I decided to buy what I could afford. I paid all my furniture with cash. I remember my first red sofa which I bought second hand for three hundred SEK (about thirty Euros).

My first ten years in Sweden were intensively dominated by many things. These included things like; getting established in the new country, learning the new language, understanding the culture and the people, studying, working, dealing with all sorts of fear, and struggling with relationships. In addition to all these, like many immigrants, I had to frequently send money to my family in Uganda for education and healthcare services. The life strategies that I learnt from my childhood were extremely useful at this point.

After about three years in Sweden, my mother caught HIV/AIDS and finally died at the age of forty-six. It was only two weeks after I had left Uganda to cater for her treatment and assist her in different ways. I am grateful that I was there before she died. I had the opportunity to talk with her, and she told me, "Sarah, remember your responsibility to take care of your younger siblings." It was painful for me not to attend my mother's burial ceremony. I could not afford to pay for both travel and burial ceremony expenses. Instead, I sent money for the burial ceremony. My colleagues at work collected money as a way of extending their kind condolences to me, for which I was grateful. Burial ceremonies in Uganda are highly respected and can get pretty expensive.

My unknown father came to haunt me after my grandmother and mother died. When I visited Uganda in 2001, I started the investigation about my father. I was told to check in a school 80 kilometres away in eastern Uganda. I remember asking every staff member at that school, and nobody seemed to know who he was. I never succeeded to find my father or knowing anything about him or his relatives. The other half of me remains a mystery, which makes me mysterious. As many people would be blaming their childhood challenges for failures in adulthood, I refuse to associate my adult challenges with my unknown father.

Making My Way into Higher Education in Sweden

I came to Sweden full of energy and hopes, with a top-university degree in economics. I felt I was on top of the world, as I belonged to the exclusive club of educated elites. However, it did not seem to matter in my new country. After I was granted the residence and work permit I sent my Ugandan university education to the Swedish Higher Education Authority for evaluation. It was confirmed to be equivalent to a Swedish Bachelor of Science in Economics. I thought that I would quickly continue with higher education in Sweden. I sent applications to universities to enrol in Master's or PhD programmes in economics but only received negative responses.

The programme I was enrolled in by the Agency of Employment Services while at the post office was a one-year programme in business administration and computer skills for immigrants with university education. This program included a trainee period of three months at a working place. The programme was led by efficient managers who were genuinely committed to getting us into trainee programmes that would lead to employment. I was introduced to Professor Kristina Orth-Gomér at the Institute of Psychosocial Medicine at Karolinska Institutet (KI) by one of the managers - Assar Byström. I was blessed to be accepted to embark on a three months' training with Kristina. It was great timing. Kristina had just started a unique project on women and coronary heart disease. Kristina was an amazing physician and an entrepreneur who was excellent at tapping into unproven talents. I was focused on giving my very best to Kristina. I quickly proved to her loyalty, hard work, high performance, and eagerness to learn new things. Kristina saw in me a potential scientist. She offered me a job as a research assistant to create the new database for the whole project. I was thrilled!

I wanted to learn more about medical statistics and to master the use of statistical packages for carrying out analyses. So I decided to study biostatistics, and I successfully got enrolled for a master's degree in biostatistics at the Department of Statistics at Stockholm University. Kristina was incredibly generous, and she enabled me to attend lectures during the day.

However, I was temporarily registered until I had passed Swedish language level three. I had previously attended lessons for Swedish as a second language, where I discovered that the class had a mixture of all kinds of people with different levels of education, including those who could not read or write. I was impatient and anxious to learn the Swedish language very quickly, as I knew that it was a fundamental key for me to successfully integrate into this new society. I decided to drop out of the class and learn on my own. I read children's books and newspapers, chatted with other Swedish people, listened to the radio, and watched American movies on Swedish television which were translated with Swedish subtitles.

I passed all the exams at the university, and I started to collect data for my master's thesis which I finished before any other student in the class. I had no trouble understanding the Swedish language in class. The mathematical formulas were after all not so different. In the exams, I elaborated my answers in English, and I am very grateful for the flexibility of the teachers and for the support at the Department of Statistics. All my points from the exams were recorded, but I was not yet formally registered, as I didn't have time to do the required Swedish exams. I was advised that I could get a dispensation if I publicly defended my master's thesis in Swedish. I practiced fiercely and eloquently defending my master's thesis publicly in Swedish. I passed, and I was awarded a master's degree in biostatistics.

I was now ready to embark on my PhD research studies. Kristina had laid out an impressive hypothetical model on how to evaluate factors for cardiovascular risks among women. Given my insights about socioeconomic conditions, I believed in the hypothesis that socioeconomic factors would potentially be associated with increased risk for coronary heart disease. It's upon this hypothesis that I developed my research plan for doctoral studies. It took me less than four years to finalize my doctoral studies.

Kristina enabled me to go for further training in epidemiology and health economics at other universities in the United States, UK, and Sweden. She also enabled me to participate in various international scientific conferences and to work with talented scientists from other top universities. I am very grateful for all these great opportunities which gave me the opportunity to learn and grow as a scientist and as a person.

At the beginning of my doctoral studies, I was introduced to a Ugandan man who was studying art sciences in Germany (we call him Pante). Pante later joined me in Sweden. Shortly after, I had my first beautiful daughter Erina. Pante's integration in Sweden was slow, and he became passive-aggressive while my scientific career was skyrocketing. The four years during my doctoral studies were hard. My mother had died, my siblings needed my support, I was in a bad relationship, taking care of Erina and dealing with tough workplace politics. Many things were against me. However, I was driven more than ever before to reach my goal – attaining my PhD within four years. I extended my timeframe and slept only four hours every day for a couple of years. I cherished the power of mind and all I learnt in Uganda. I was like a machine: I had a lot of energy and never felt exhausted.

On 12 February 1999, I defended my PhD thesis on social and psychosocial risk factors for cardiovascular diseases in women. The examination board consisted of the best public health scientists, and several people attended my PhD defence. My thesis had a great media attraction, and I was on national television (for the first time) to tell about my findings. Unlike many PhD graduates who celebrate with big parties, inviting family, relatives, colleagues, and friends, I did not have good reasons for throwing a party. I was missing my mother and grandmother. Most sadly, I had just discovered that my daughter Erina suffered from a serious disability. Kristina organized an incredible lunch party at the department with the support of kind colleagues.

The graduation party at the Stockholm city hall, three months after my defence, made me feel so happy and grateful. However, I missed my mother and my grandmother that evening.

Sarah Wamala Andersson, PhD

(Photo of Sarah at the graduation ceremony
at Stockholm city hall, May 1999)

Experiences with my Daughter's Disabilities

An unexpected turning point came when my daughter Erina was diagnosed as suffering from autism and developmental disorders. After my PhD, I was offered a post doctoral research position at the University of Michigan, with attractive benefits. It was my dream to carry out research in the United States. However, I found out that the insurance package would not cover therapies related to Erina's disabilities, as they were regarded as pre-existing conditions. I was a single mum by then, and I could not see how I could cater for Erina's treatment in a way that would effectively enhance her development. I turned down the postdoc offer, and I was devastated. I decided to focus on Erina's interventions.

My mind was preoccupied with questions such as; how could this happen to my daughter when it was only one in a thousand children that would be diagnosed as suffering from autism? What caused this? How would my daughter be cured? I decided to dedicate my time and energy to finding the cure for Erina. I started the long journey of digging into the autism research and personal stories. These helped me to find programmes and interventions that helped to progress Erina's development.

Everything ranging from the sorrow of losing the child of my dreams to fighting for resources for interventions and doing everything possible for Erina left me exhausted. I had never heard of the word "autism" until I started to read books in the search for answers to why Erina was not responding as other children did at her kindergarten. The first book that opened my eyes was edited by a British psychiatrist, Lorna Wing, *The Autistic Spectrum: A Guide for Parents and Professionals* (1996). In the introductory chapter, she described a boy named Peter who suffered from autism and developmental disorders. The description of Peter left me with no doubt that my daughter was in big trouble.

The next challenge was to acquire a medical diagnosis for Erina. It was a long queue of about two years. I was impatient and angry. I wrote fifty letters to every manager in the Stockholm County Council requesting to schedule for Erina's diagnostic procedures. I finally got an appointment to start the diagnostic procedures for Erina. I remember painfully when the diagnosis was set that Erina, four and a half years old, suffered from infantile autism and developmental disorders.

To add salt to my wounded heart, the physician told me,

"I can imagine that this may feel painful for you, given the fact that you have attained the highest educational level, but your daughter will never be able to read or write. In fact, Erina will never be able to learn anything at all. She will spend most of her life in institutions, and she will not be able to live a normal life."

The physician was right that this was very painful for me. However, this made me fiercely angry enough to make sure that Erina's life becomes better than predicted.

In the meantime, my relationship with Pante was not good at all. Additionally, Pante chose to refuse to acknowledge that Erina had a serious disability and that she needed immediate interventions. I wanted to pay undivided attention to finding Erina's cure, and I didn't have time for nonsense or unnecessary distractions. I made radical changes to provide my daughter with effective interventions at an early age. I bought my first apartment in the inner city where resources were available for Erina's interventions. I divorced Pante. Since then, Pante chose to "play dead". Erina has no idea about her biological father. In fact, my husband, Per, whom I met when Erina was about five years old, has been the real father of Erina. Per is the only father that Erina knows until this day.

Erina has a great life. She is happy and content. Erina learned to swim independently at the age of nine. She learned to read and write at the age of ten. She learned to manage her daily life at eleven. She learned to take care of her menstrual periods right from the beginning at the age of twelve. Erina is good at computers, and she started them at the age of three. She is a big fan of iPhones, and she enjoys music. She plays guitar and drums, and she has a beautiful singing voice. Erina is now twenty years old, and she takes a metro by herself to and from school which is about 15 kilometres away from her home.

Erina's progress is a result of various things. Erina's younger sister, Nellie, and my husband, Per, have meant a great deal for Erina's progress, and they have been my great enablers. I am incredibly grateful for the wonderful people who have worked with Erina and for the support from family, relatives, and friends over the years. Collaboration with schools, local governments, various networks and public policies have played a substantial role.

Erina's progress is another example of how higher education matters in daily life. My research training has been beneficial in understanding the scientific literature and interpreting the findings to understand autism and identify effective treatments and programmes to enhance Erina's development.

Twenty years with Erina have been a great learning experience for my family and me. I gratefully perceive Erina as a gift to me. I believe that my experiences with Erina have made me a better person. This is why I want to share my experiences by giving opportunities to children like Erina to live a more meaningful and happier life. This is why we initiated Abilities Beyond Boarders (ABeBO) on Erina's twentieth birthday, November 2015. The aim of ABeBo is to establish schools for children with autism spectrum disorders (ASD) in Africa, to reduce stigmatization and to provide opportunities for exchange of knowledge beyond boarders.

I am grateful to Carina Hoijar, one of Erina's teachers, who has taught me that we should be talking about 'variations in abilities' instead of 'disabilities'.

> I believe that the story about my experiences with my daughter Erina and her varying abilities deserve its own space in another book!

My Family

After several years of hard work and caring for my daughter Erina, I decided to redefine my goals including the type of relationships I wanted to invest in. I wanted to become a better me and design my life in a more desirable fushion. My first strategy was to set goals for Erina's intervention programmes and my career (including determining the level of salary I wanted to earn). I advanced fast in my career. I won the prestigious Knut and Alice Wallenberg prize for talented young women scientists which made it easier for me to get promoted as associate professor and senior lecturer (only three years after my PhD studies). I felt that I had created a stable base for me and my daughter, and I was ready to find love that I deserved.

I thought through carefully what love meant to me and what qualities I wanted to see in a man who I would eventually share my life with. I started with writing down a list of qualities that I didn't appreciate, and another list of the qualities that I appreciated. The lists included having Erina as my number-one priority. I dated a couple of successful, nice, and energetic guys. Among these guys, Per was the one who captured my heart and turned out to be the best fit for Erina and me. Per is an incredibly handsome, caring, and fine man who came to be a real father to Erina. It is amazing that when you clearly decide on what you want and make a plan, you actually get it.

After a couple of years, Per and I were blessed with a beautiful and talented girl, Nellie. We gave her "Robinah" as her middle name to honour my grandmother. Nellie is so smart and intuitive, just like my grandmother. Per and I have had totally different lives, yet we share similar fundamental values. When I met Per, he had never been to any country outside Europe, and he had no friends with immigrant backgrounds. Per joined me on a trip to Uganda in 2002 which was a life-changing moment for him. I remember the first time Per's parents invited me to dinner and how nervous he was about their responses. Like Per, his parents were rarely exposed to people with other backgrounds. I had braided my hair and Per's mother secretly admired my hair but didn't ask any questions. Given my African background where family and friends play a big role, I am keen on keeping a good relationship with Per's parents, siblings, and relatives.

In spite of living in Sweden, my role as the eldest sibling to mentor and support my younger siblings and their families is still relevant. I have two siblings in Uganda (Ritah and Fred), one in the UK (Edith), and another one in South Africa (Gift). Two other siblings passed on. I am very close to my sisters – they are incredible. Their children have become smart young people, and they also depend on me to mentor, coach, and support them in different ways. My focus is on educational attainment and the right mindset.

I have also acquired close friends who are almost like family to me. I appreciate them.

Making My Way into a Scientific and Professional Career in Sweden

The timing of my doctoral thesis was perfect. This was the time when scientists and policymakers wanted to know more about women's health and socioeconomic implications on health. Because of the medial exposure of my doctoral thesis, my research became known by others. It is the doctoral training that paved my professional success. Gunnar Ågren participated in one of the seminars where I presented my research findings, just before he became the director general of the Swedish National Institute of Health in Stockholm. He had a task of integrating scientific findings with public health practice, and he needed to recruit people with research training. I was hired at the institute as a research manager. I wanted to use my research training to contribute to better population health. It is at the institute where my skills in public health policies, civil service, public administration, and management were developed and shaped. Additionally, the institute gave me further learning experiences related to workplace politics. I was the first person with an African background to work at the institute, and I am grateful to many colleagues who were open-minded and supportive.

Gunnar, just like Kristina, saw my potential, and he was convinced that the institute benefited from having me on board. Gunnar was an incredibly supportive executive who enabled me to grow as a public health scientist, a civil servant, and as a leader. I had the opportunity to embark on my managerial career, work on important projects, present the Swedish public health at various international scientific conferences. Additionally I had the opportunity to work as a guest scientist at Wellington School of Medicine in New Zealand. My family and I had a great time in New Zealand, and I learnt a lot from excellent colleagues there with whom I published a paper on twenty-year trends of social inequalities in premature death. I was thrilled. In New Zealand, there was no moment when I felt reminded that being black was undesirable. It was amazing to experience how people in New Zealand treated everyone (including my children and me) equally well.

After about eight incredible years at the institute, I was head-hunted by a recruiting firm and hired as a director of a department of health promotin and disease promotion at the Stockholm County Council. I appreciate the significant role that recruiting firms and managers play when it comes to identifying people with (unobvious) high potential and talents and finally hire them.

Appointment as Director General

I served as a director on the council for less than two years. On 31st July 2008, the Swedish government appointed me as the director general of the Swedish National Institute of Public Health (the highest level for civil servants in Sweden).

I was the first person with an African background ever to achieve such a position. Looking back from where my life started in Kituntu, who would even hypothesize that a girl with humble beginnings from a rural village in Uganda would be the first person with African background to earn a position as a director general in Sweden? This is a good example how high education in addition to purposefully believing in your self can pay off in various ways.

I was on an afternoon walk with my family in the beautiful Stockholm archipelago when the minister of public health called me on my cell phone. I listened carefully while trembling and wondering whether I had heard correctly. The minister said to me, "The Swedish Government has made a decision to hire the most competent person as the new director general of the Swedish National Institute of Public Health, and that person is you, Sarah." The minister asked me, "Will you take the job?"

I felt my stomach ache, and I sat down on the roadside, but I could not give any immediate answer. I kindly asked the minister if I could think through and get back in a few days. I called the minister a day later and thanked for the offer. It felt great. I was perplexed that my appointment had an extensive media attraction. The newspapers headlines run as follows: "The First Person with African Background To Be Appointed as Director General". The profile included having attained a PhD and managerial experience. I had these at hand when the opportunity came and education mattered.

Positions as director general in Sweden were now open for public application for the first time. Nevertheless, I could not imagine that I would be considered for such a position. In fact, I was encouraged by one of my mentors to apply for the position, as I fulfilled all the requirements. At first, I hesitated, but finally, I decided to apply for the position. My goal was to show the Swedish government that I was interested in such positions and I had what it took. I was impressed by the professionalism and integrity of the recruiting firm that had the task of recruiting director generals. The task included finding eligible candidates, interviewing them, and presenting a short list to the minister. I enjoyed and learned a lot from the whole process. I also learned not to let fear stand in my way and to always aim much higher.

During this process, my brother (Moses, thirty years) who lived in South Africa was brutally murdered by robbers. I was devastated, and I was not able to concentrate. Besides the pain of losing my brother, I had to help with a number of logistics back in Uganda related to finding his body, a burial ceremony, and many other things.

While serving as director general, I was keen on becoming a great leader, growing personally, and supporting my team. Learning more and becoming better every day is part of who I am. In addition to the research education, I have invested in acquiring the best knowledge in leadership and management skills. I was blessed to be one of the few women executives who were enrolled in the very first Swedish national programme for executive board skills. I was the only woman with African background among the 740 women who participated in the programme for executive board skills from 2009 to 2014.

I have participated in several top international leadership development programmes, including the Stanford executive programme at the Stanford Business Graduate School in the United States. I am grateful for such a great opportunity to acquire incredible knowledge in business management from the prestigious Stanford University. Learning from the great Stanford professors and exchanging knowledge and experiences with top executives from different parts of the world was amazing and empowering. I am a life member of the Stanford Business School Alumni Association, unbelievable!

My thirst to learn more and add more value has contributed to an extraordinary growth for me as a person and a leader, which has enabled me to support others and increase performance. I was blessed to work with colleagues at the institute who were dedicated to improving people's health, and to see them grow as excellent public health officials and leaders. I am proud of the incredible work that we accomplished together to make people's lives better.

Persisting to Achieve the Highest Academic Professional Title

After attaining my PhD in 1999, my goal was to go all the way and hold the title of professor. Again, at that time I had no idea how my professional journey was going to turn out. Nevertheless, I was promoted as associate professor three years after my PhD. When I became the director general, a former PhD colleague told me (buzzing), "Now we take different paths —you become a director general, and I become a professor," as if she knew what my goal was. She actually meant that I would never become a professor as it was almost impossible to fulfil the academic portfolio demands of achieving a professorship while holding a highly intensive administrative job. I felt challenged by this, as I had always wanted to achieve the highest academic title of professor. I made a decision to pursue the title of professor. I was aware of my capacity and how much I could stretch it. I knew I could do it. I studied and understood what was required to become a professor at Karolinska Institutet. The requirements included teaching, supervising at least two PhD students to final dissertation, publishing several scientific articles in international peer-reviewed scientific journals, publishing textbooks, practicing leadership practice, and implementing science into practice.

I decided to make it a hobby to fill up my academic portfolio using the little leisure time I had. It was actually productive for my tasks as a director general because I kept pace with current research.

The evaluation process to be promoted to a full professor at KI is exhaustingly long. The process took me almost two years, and I almost gave up. But I was determined to reach my goal. In April 2014, I became a professor of health policy and leadership. I finally earned the highest academic recognition. On 17 October 2014, I was formally installed as a professor in a very beautiful and high-level ceremony. Standing there in the beautiful KI's Aula, together with other twenty new professors, felt like a dream that had really come true. I was the only person with African descent among the professors that were installed 2014.

Again on this day, I missed the presence of my mother and my grandmother as they pushed me to the edges to pursue higher education. It was incredible looking at a photo (where I was highlighted) announcing new professors on KI's website.

I appreciate the research training which provided me with opportunities of working and publishing with great scientists from different parts of the world and learning from them. Teaching and discussing with students and thinking critically provided a great learning opportunity.

(Photo of Sarah at the professor installation ceremony
at Karolinska Institute, October 2014)

Sharing Learned Lessons

I have learnt enormously in my journey from where it started in Kituntu to where I am now in Stockholm. What is it that has contributed to my perseverance to overcome challenges, thrive, and finally succeed? How has my higher education from Uganda helped me to tap into opportunities to live a better life and turn obstacles into possibilities in the new country?

Higher education has been an excellent tool for me to be able to live a better life. However, I have learnt that it is not education per se, but it is in combination with other things that I have been able to effectively tap into opportunities along the way. Other things include; who I am and my vision to make a difference, how I was raised, what I have learned through experiences and from others, and a strong drive to constantly move forward.

I have developed a mindset which includes a combination of a burning desire to become better and greater every day, strong faith in higher powers, a high dose of positivity and to add value. I am my own competition and I don't compete with others. I believe that competing with other people reduces both my own and others' unique qualities.

I am aware of the multiple burdens that I face daily, but I do not allow these to distract me. I don't let circumstances control my life. I know that I have to perform way beyond average; therefore, I set very high goals. I believe in the power within me and in the guidance of higher powers to achieve my goals and realize my dreams. I practice maintaining an internal peace. I am constantly grateful and I attempt to interpret negative experiences as learning opportunities.

Whether I like it or not, I realise that most of the time, other people want to remind me that being a black person is an obstacle. This happens regardless of where I am or what I am doing. It can be when walking down the street or when participating in high-level meetings with well-accomplished people from different parts of the world. There is no doubt that being black and a woman poses a double burden; nevertheless, I refuse to let this belief dominate my thoughts or distract me. I believe that with higher education, the right mindset, and the strong belief in the higher powers and the power that comes from within, many of the obstacles can be turned into opportunities.

I have gratefully learned from my daughter Erina and others that every human being is unique, and have a special purpose to uniquely contribute to the world. The difference is that we all see the world differently. This way of thinking guides me to respect every person and attempt to focus on their positive attributes.

Thanks to my higher education and life experiences, I attempt to find solutions to every problem using learned analytical skills and creativity. I believe that problems are there to be solved or learn from them and not to whine about them. I read extensively, and I look out for informal professional mentors and coaches, whom I highly appreciate. I am interested in sharing what I learn with other people, as this creates a reciprocal learning.

Higher education helps me to efficiently read and critically analyse intensive materials and easily understand the environment and the people around me. I have been invited to participate in high-level meetings and in important projects in different parts of the world. I have travelled extensively to great places, and I have met incredible people. I am convinced with no education (that given my humble beginnings and being a black person), I would not have experienced many great things as I have, and my life would be much different (worse) regardless of where I lived.

I have learnt to create time and space for deep reflection and to ask myself important questions about life, questions like:

- What does success and happiness mean to me?

- What can I do to become better and greater every day?

- How can I efficiently use my knowledge and experiences in a way that adds value to me and to others?

- How can I make a difference that creates the greatest impact to make people's lives better?

What Next?

A girl from humble beginnings in rural Kituntu in Uganda migrated to an unknown world with a university degree, a suitcase full of lousy clothes, and a hundred US dollars. Two decades later, she had built up her life from nothing to a middle-class level in Sweden. When I think about that girl, I am committed to keeping on moving forward and becoming better and greater every day. I want to believe that I didn't come this far, to only get this far. I understand that higher education by itself is not enough, but it is a great asset. I strongly believe that I can and will do much more to inspire others and to continue contributing to making people's lives better. My humble beginnings will not stop me!

Linley Chiwona-Karltun, PhD

Winners never quit and quitters never win
Vince Lombardi

Black women of any origin need to know their worth.
Don't let other people define your worth.
Inspired by 20 Feet from Stardom – the
background singers in music history

Linley Chiwona-Karltun, PhD

Acknowledgements

This story is dedicated to the next generation of African-Swedes,
especially my daughters Karin and Nora

Inspired by my father, who died too soon
at seventy-four years in 2011,

To my dearest friend Beatrice Chaika Winnberg for
patiently being there during this writing process,

To you who made a difference in my life,

And to Erik, my lifelong partner, whose words
of wisdom made this story what is

That Thing Called School

In 1993, an opportunity much unexpected presented itself, a glimmer of hope to undertake my PhD studies. I was asked if I spoke any of the local languages in Malawi and if I would consider going back there. At the time, Malawi was still under the draconian rule of the late president for life Ngwazi Dr Hastings Kamuzu Banda. With much trepidation, I wondered if it would be safe for me to travel back to Malawi after fourteen years of pretty much living in fear of perhaps saying the wrong thing to someone, maybe a spy who could jeopardise my family's safety. I had left Malawi with my family because my father, Peter Chiwona, who was an accomplished academician, was persecuted by the Banda regime. He was born in Chitipa, north Malawi, whose insular regional politics had permeated and continues to permeate all levels of society. What a shame, really, because this has resulted in unnecessary contestations, particularly in the area of higher education. This is part of my story, the story of how, propelled by my father with the strong belief that I had the talent to excel in school, I beat the odds and tenaciously sought and attained higher education.

For most of my life growing up in Malawi, I had been surrounded by uncles and aunties who had achieved accolades in their respective education. Some were lawyers, economists, educationists, agricultural scientists, specialised medical doctors, nurses, home economists, and teachers ranging from primary schools to universities. It was basically expected that I would also follow in those footsteps because I was, after all, Peter Chiwona's daughter and the granddaughter of NyaMbisa Shakuyoba. Anyone with Mbisa blood in them had to get highly educated. Yes, in some families in Malawi, a girl in the 1960s was expected not only to attend primary and secondary school but also to get a bachelor's degree and to excel well beyond a bachelor's degree. And of course, she also had to get married, but that is another story for another book. So as you can imagine, the opportunity to engage in possible doctoral studies truly outweighed the risk of probably being in trouble if I travelled back to Malawi. After all these years, here was an opportunity to study further and to fulfil the great family tradition. With an eight-and-a-half-month old baby and still breastfeeding, I began my preparations for the field trip to Malawi. Firstly, I needed a breast pump to express breast milk for freezing so that while I was away, the baby's father, Erik, could continue to breastmilk feed our daughter Karin. Secondly, my husband had to plan for paternity leave to take care of his daughter for the period that I would be away. Thirdly, a backup network of family and friends was rallied up to support my being away for three weeks. The network was a strong group of women, my mother-in-law, Ingrid; my foster mother, Rosa; and in Malawi my own mother, Irene Makwegho. This band of women was to be the alpha and the omega, an expression we used a lot while studying in secondary school, of my never-failing backup plan for completing my doctoral studies. These women, I believe, were indirectly also living their dreams of pursuing higher education and careers in academia – how could I possibly fail them?

Going to school and being well read was non-negotiable with my parents. It did not matter whether it was school time or holiday times; throughout my childhood, my father and mother expected us to read every day. Our house was always filled with books, and each day we were expected to have read something that we could tell our father about when he came back from work in the evening. And, boy did my mother see to it that we read! With a stern look on her face and a telling off if you did not do as told, the afternoons were mostly spent sitting quietly in a chair reading for at least two hours. Even when my father could afford to buy us a television, my family did not own a television until 1980. When he eventually bought a television, my father made sure that the films we saw on VHS were educational ones, like Shakespeare and, naturally, *The Sound of Music*. Every evening after having taken a bath and eaten dinner, all of us sat quietly in the living room with a book in hand. When I look back, I realise that this is what helped me so much in acquiring a habit of reading and a zest for disappearing into books. I have had my name called a couple of times at the airport while browsing through books as I totally lose track of time.

With my father being the first in his family to go beyond secondary school and on to university, it was expected that after completing secondary school, the next logical step for me would be university. Alas, this was not to be that simple, because my father was persecuted and eventually imprisoned, and the family had to flee Malawi when I was only seventeen years old. The move to Ethiopia was not that simple, and again my father made a decisive decision to leave me and my brother Lekani behind in Malawi so that we could finish our secondary school education. As always my father had done his education research about schools in Ethiopia. He had found out that the English education system in Ethiopia at the time was not as well-developed as in Malawi, especially for upper secondary school studies. I was scared to be left behind, but it was this being left behind that made me realise just how much my father valued education and that I had to do well in school.

(Peter Chiwona at seventy years sporting his Oxford scarf, in his garden in Mzuzu and being paid respect by the many young men who he mentored over the years; Photo: courtesy of his daughter, Linley)

So the rest of my family moved to Ethiopia where my parents worked and lived for nineteen years. Meanwhile, I successfully completed my secondary school education in form three and form four. Despite having achieved good grades in form four to pursue university studies in Malawi, I was not selected to pursue college degree studies, but I was selected to pursue secretarial studies. My father would simply not hear of it. Allow his daughter to pursue a profession so synonymous with women? Oh no! He had bigger dreams for me, and nothing would get in his way. Without really knowing what next, I only knew that I would continue with school somehow. At the same time, I felt like such a failure. *Why was I not selected to go to university like my school friends, given my good grades? When*, I asked myself, *will my northern origins and the last name Chiwona cease to be a hindrance?* Being in Ethiopia as a foreigner during the Derg Mengistu regime in the eighties had its own challenges. There was limited opportunity for pursuing post-secondary school studies in English. To study outside Ethiopia would have meant having your own finances and plenty of them. As an exiled family, I was not eligible for scholarships that required endorsement from the Malawi government.

Peter Chiwona was a man of many talents, and one of them was his ever-searching mind and strong social competence. He had friends from all walks of life, and this taught me much about how to network. Before I knew it, my dad had "fixed" a school in the UK. My dad was somewhat of a fixer – he fixed things, and most of the time, he used his analytical mathematical mind to fix things.

In 1980, I went to study my advanced-level studies at Our Lady's Convent, Alnwick, in Northumberland, England. The boarding school accommodation was located in Baliffgate, the same quarters as the now-famous Alnwick Castle were Harry Potter and the movie *Elizabeth* was filmed. This was a no-nonsense school run by Irish nuns belonging to the Sisters of Mercy. Although I had attended several international and predominantly white schools during my primary and secondary school studies, I was still taken aback by being in England. Imagine: I was in

England, wearing my new platform shoes bought in Mercato market in Addis Ababa and with my big afro. I was finally in the same league as those had "been abroad".

It was not all excitement. I was also quite nervous about being in England. What if I got lost? There were so many new things. A week before I was to appear at school, my father and mother spent one week with me and my eight-year-old sister Tina and nine-year-old brother Pierre. My father was sending all three of us to English boarding schools in the UK at the same time.

The first week my sister and I attended Our Lady's Convent High School there was an incident with the boarders. Somebody had urinated on the floor in the toilets, and the nuns were going to get to the bottom of this. I was called to the headmistress's office with my little sister and asked if we knew how to use a flushing water closet. I really do not know where I got the courage from, but the earlier days of schooling and being a minority in the schools in Malawi came rushing back.

"Yes, sister," I replied. "In fact, we have been attending English boarding schools before coming here." There and then, I knew I had to take on my Sir Harry Johnston primary school role, no nonsense.

My father was determined to see to it that we got things right from the start, and he gave us a crash course that I refer to as "UK-101: How to Quickly Survive in London." Here is a very short version of it, and do remember that this was the time before Internet and mobile phones were common place.

> *If you are lost in London, just look for a tube station, and get on the circle line— it will always keep going round and round. Use the time on the circle line to study the map and plan your journey. Learn to appreciate Chinese takeaway; it is cheap and tasty, and you can always find something to eat. Of course, stroll down Oxford Circus and Piccadilly Square but beware of the prices – best you go to*

> *Shepherd's Bush to buy similar things for lower prices. Visit*
> *the museums, the British Museum, and Madame Tussauds*
> *to get a deeper understanding of British history, because*
> *then you will understand how Britain worked.*

My father was a man who appreciated the creative arts, and during that one week, he made sure that he took us to the West End theatre. I will never forget the first time my father took us to watch *My Fair Lady*. It remains my favourite musical theatre.

The politics of Margaret Thatcher in the eighties in Britain made school tuition exorbitantly expensive and impossible for me to think of pursuing self-sponsored university studies. Without any nomination for any form of government-approved scholarships, together with my father, we had to think of a new strategy for pursing university studies. This was a trying period for me. I kept in touch with some of my old classmates, now in university. Here I was with my graduation certificate and no university. My father did not want to see me idle, so he encouraged me to look for some activities that could keep me occupied while we searched for university options.

The first thing that I tried was learning to type. I thought it might come in handy, in case I never made it to college. The second thing that my father thought would be good for me was learning to drive. I had never seen so many women driving cars as I did in Ethiopia in the early eighties. My mother had learned how to drive, and now it was my turn. The wonderful thing about learning to drive in Ethiopia was that you simply went to Revolution Square and there was a whole parking lot of Volkswagen Beetles with a driver ready to give you a lesson. I believe it costed five Ethiopian birr per hour at the time.

Choosing a university or college in the United States was a whole science by itself. The sizes alone were overwhelming, and I wondered if I could study on a campus with more than twenty thousand students. My idea of big was simply not this size. When I was younger, I used to kneel and pray to God to make sure that I lived up to twenty years and now this. Really, what sort of buildings did they have to cater for so many students? The second factor I had to consider was the tuition fees: just how much could we afford to pay? The third consideration was the ranking of the college in terms of competitiveness and scholastic achievement. In Malawi, just by saying which school you were selected to for your secondary school studies indicated how well you had scored or how bright you were.

I have been greatly influenced by my father's love of the arts and literature. Very early in my life, I established an interest in English literature, especially William Shakespeare and drama. While attending my secondary school years, I seriously took up drama, encouraged by my English teacher who was a Peace Corps volunteer from the United States. I have to admit that while the political environment was stifling in Malawi, education quality flourished. Our drama teacher informed us that she had registered our school for the national best school play competition. She chose a play where the main actor was a strong African woman, and I was selected for that role. I memorised my lines and took on, I would say, the most important role in my short-lived acting career. Our school won the regional competition in the north, and we went on to the finals in Lilongwe. I simply loved being on stage and acting out. The night when we had to perform our play, remembering all the tips and coaching from my teacher, I put on my best act. While our play did not win the national trophy, I was awarded the prize for best diction, a book titled *Out of the Silent Planet* by C.S. Lewis. And so my dream to become an actress by profession was born.

Oh, how I loved acting! But my father, a realist in life, simply said, "Over my dead body." This was an expression that, as kids, we would bet each other to see if he would say it or not. My father never hit us when we were growing up, but when he said *no*, that was it. But I was a stubborn child, and I would always ask why not when he said no.

"Because," he said, "You can never make a career out of it, not in Malawi." *In that case*, I said to myself, *I will try to do it elsewhere.* I think this was the beginning of my coming to the realisation that if I could not do something there and then, well then, I had to find another way of doing it.

Having been told that I could not pursue an acting career, I threw myself into my next passion, cooking. After all, as a girl in Malawi, it was expected that I help out in the kitchen with cooking and cleaning, whether in the village or in town. It is this that lead to my second interest in domestic science with a keen interest in baking. I loved to see things being mixed together and then watching them come out as new products. I really did not want to become a teacher, but I wondered if one could pursue further studies in these subjects and specialise on the subject in university. As I looked through the university guidebook, I would come across the words "food nutrition" and "dietetics". Without the Internet in those days, the Oxford dictionary was my greatest companion. I was drawn to this subject and set about applying to universities for these studies.

In the end, I accepted an offer to study at East Carolina University (ECU), a constituent college of North Carolina State University in Greenville North Carolina. It was not a big city. The university offered a professional programme in food nutrition and institutional management, and they had a programme in English literature, yes, Shakespearean tragedies! Upon registration, I was to learn that acceptance to the programme was conditional, and I had to formally apply again after completing forty-four course-credit points of the compulsory prerequisites with a minimum of 2.5 grade-point average. If I did not make the grade, I could wave goodbye to the dream, and what would my parents say given all the sacrifices they had made to send me that far in quest of higher education?

When I arrived in the United States, I found a new environment at ECU so different from Britain. There were all sorts of people – from Africa,

60

Asia, Europe, Latin America, and, yes, different parts of the States. As an international student, ECU was exceptional in taking care of its foreign students, with a special house called the International House where students could meet together, watch telly, and share experiences. It was here that I learned that it was possible to get on-campus employment while studying. Equipped with this knowledge, I set about looking for a job, not just one but two jobs, and at times, I even had three jobs.

The good thing about studying in the United States is that depending on what you choose to study you could be employed as a laboratory assistant, teaching assistant, waitress, auditorium usher, or other off-campus opportunities such as babysitting or as a chamber maid in hotels. Hard work, commitment, and honesty gave me more jobs than I could cope with. The tuition was paid for by my father because he worked with the United Nations Economic Commission for Africa (UNECA), but the money for housing, food, books, and other things that I wished to enjoy came from me through the many jobs I worked.

Balancing working with studies required a lot of discipline with little time for wiling the hours away. Still, I made the time to go for happy hour on Fridays and keg bash parties, though I never did acquire the taste for beer. My favourite drinks were margaritas and daiquiris, and I probably drank one too many then, as I do not care for them as much anymore.

My passion for drama continued, but this time, I took courses in English literature with a focus on the Shakespeare tragedies. In my extracurricular activities with the International Student Association, I became the entertainment director, a position I created to act out my fantasies of being an actress.

While studying in the United States, I was often confronted with a deep longing for home, for Africa. The famine in Ethiopia in 1984–5 made that longing even stronger, but it also made me question my focus in my studies. Did I really want to work as a dietician, counselling patients with obesity, hypertension, and coronary heart disease? It became increasingly clear to me that problems of poverty and hunger captured my interest much more. So I started to investigate about what it would take for me to work with poverty and food shortage. One thing became very clear: there would be a need to pursue further studies to understand problems of poverty and hunger. Further studies meant getting a master's degree, and I was intrigued by the possibility of studying public health and tropical medicine. Being in the United States had brought me much closer with Latin America and being in the United States brought me closer to working as a volunteer in development issues. To be accepted for graduate school studies in the United States, I needed to sit for the Graduate Record Examination (GRE). Being so passionate about this new interest, I went about studying for the GRE, paid the fees, and sat for the examination. Concurrently, I applied to several colleges offering such studies, and I received three offers. I accepted the offer from the prestigious Tulane School of Public Health and Tropical Medicine in Louisiana. But this was not to be, the tuition fees were beyond my budget. My father had made one commitment to each one of his children. He would be responsible for our tuition only up to the first degree, and any one of us wishing to pursue further studies would have to fend for oneself. By now, I was beginning to wonder if the United States was the only place to pursue my postgraduate studies. To think about this, I asked Tulane University if they could defer my offer to the following year, which they kindly accepted. I left the United States for Ethiopia with two very clear aims. One was to look for possibilities of studying the same programme where I could get some financial support, and the second was to get work that could enable me to save money for tuition. I received offers from the London School of Hygiene and Tropical Medicine and the University of Queensland Australia. At one time, I was even shortlisted for development studies at Cambridge University. But I was not dissuaded; instead, I set about working as a volunteer with NGOs in Ethiopia to get experience and a deeper understanding of poverty and hunger issues.

One day, I happened to be visiting a clinic for some ailment, and in the waiting room, there was a fine-looking gentleman giving me that look. The look that says, "I like you." I smiled pleasantly; after all, I was brought up to have good manners as a girl. He told me that he worked with public health. That really tweaked my interest. I was on the lookout for a job, a serious job. I agreed to meet with this gentleman, and I must to this day thank him and my instincts for the opportunity. He introduced me to my first real professional job with an international organization and a salary that was the envy of many people. Because I lived at home with my parents, I saved every single penny of it towards my studies. Of course, this gentleman would remind me every once in a while how much he liked me; I would politely decline his advances. He was in a position of power, and I was beholden to him for the job. In order not to jeopardise my job, I made sure that I kept my contact with him only on a professional level.

So one evening while I was home alone, I heard a knock on the door, and this gentleman was standing outside the door, asking that I let him in. He had found out where I lived and knew that my parents were not at home. Fortunately, the house guard realized that this was not a visitor that I was expecting, and he kept hovering about, making the gentleman uncomfortable, and eventually he left. When I came to work the next day, he avoided me, and when my contract came to an end, not surprisingly, it was not renewed. At that time, I did not know that there was a term for this kind of behaviour: sexual harassment.

Ethiopia provided me with many lessons and opportunities that I am very grateful for. One of them was my chance meeting with a Swedish woman. While working in Ethiopia trying to save up money to go back to college at Tulane School of Public Health, I was introduced to the nutrition community and, more importantly, to the Swedish nutrition professional who understood my quest for higher education. This female nutrition professional began to guide me and to mentor me on how I could go about achieving my goal of getting a master's degree. During those days, much of the material for applying to study in

Sweden was in Swedish, and she painstakingly took the time to translate the application form. Together, we applied to Uppsala University in Sweden for me to pursue my master's degree in human nutrition with an emphasis on low-income countries. What really attracted me to study in Sweden was the fact that Sweden did not charge any tuition fees, even for foreign students. This has since changed as of 2011. With the savings I had from working in Ethiopia, I once again migrated from Africa to Europe, this time, Sweden, and I informed Tulane University with much regret that I would not be taking their offer.

Never before had my father or I heard of free-tuition education. Was this really true, or was it a scam? What sort of a country was this Sweden? No need to pay out-of-state tuition fees and no foreign-student fees. My father took it upon himself to find out more about whether this was indeed true, just to be sure that his daughter was not falling into some trap. With such an opportunity, what is it that could or would stop me from getting a higher education, other than my own unwillingness to do so?

But I still wanted to be sure that I was not missing out from getting a "proper British education". And so, before flying to Sweden, I bought a ticket that enabled me to stop over in London and visit the London School of Hygiene and Tropical Medicine. I was well received and met so many foreign students studying there. I had until September to make the final decision as to whether I would be able to get the money for the tuition. From the first day that I arrived in school at Uppsala University, I knew I had to anchor myself because government-funded scholarships were simply not there. I set about exploring funding opportunities equipped with a CV and knowing that the alternative could be going back to square one. A daughter of a Malawian dissident, what tools or weapon would I need for my future?

By now I had gone through quite a lot of reality issues, and I was not getting any younger. My father's responsibility had ended with my bachelor's degree. Now he simply wished me well and supported my endeavours fervently. Surely, equipped with higher education, I would have a wider playing field, as was beginning to be quite evident. Having spent much time searching for scholarships and financial aid to support my studies, I knew that I had to pursue all avenues in Sweden. Most importantly, studying in the United States at ECU had set my standards: hard work, cordiality and loyalty paid off. The American educational system is very good at equipping you with many generic skills, something I really recommend to experience.

The staff at Uppsala University was unimaginably supportive. One day, one of them, knowing my financial woes well, came with some forms to me from the Swedish Institute. We read the papers carefully together: foreign student, no permanent residence in Sweden, enrolled or invited to study at a Swedish university. More importantly, it said nothing at all about the government endorsing me for the scholarship. After all these years, I still clung to my citizenship. I did not dare to hope, because so many times, I had been so close to getting a scholarship.

In those days, a citizen of Malawi did not need a visa to come to Sweden if he or she was staying for less than three months. While the tuition was free to study in Sweden, I needed money for food, accommodation, and other amenities. My Swedish friend who had helped me to get to Sweden thought that I could get some work, but this was not as easy as in the United States. For starters, language was an issue, and there were not many foreign students or friendly work regulations for visiting students. My three months were coming to an end, and I had to renew my visa. I went to the immigration office and filled in the forms, got the regular stamp in my passport, and began the long wait for a decision.

One day, out of the blue, I received a message that my application had been denied and that I was illegally visiting Sweden. In addition, I was to leave Sweden immediately and never to enter Sweden for the coming two years. Needless to say, I was in shock. How could I be visiting Sweden illegally? I had gone to the immigration office way before my visa had run out, provided the documents showing that I was still studying, and showed them the money that I had in the bank at the time. Again, I was very lucky to have some wonderful friends who accompanied me to the immigration office to go and find out what and where I had made the mistake.

Perhaps it was my lucky day. But I am inclined to believe that there are some civil servants that really want to do right by themselves. This female police officer listened to my story, looked at the documents, and asked me to wait while she went to consult. I sat for a good while that seemed to last forever. Then she came out and said the most wonderful words that I will never forget. "It appears you have done everything correctly, so we will refer you to *rättshjälpen* (civil legal support), paid for by the Swedish State."

Again, I asked myself: what sort of country is this that makes one decision to throw you out, and then pays for you to get a lawyer that can prove that they made the wrong decision? So commenced this long process of meeting with the lawyer and writing to the immigration board.

One day when I came to the department, one of my lecturers comes smilingly at me with a letter in her hand. "Congratulations, you are the recipient of a Swedish Institute scholarship for two years!" I could not believe it! Me, Linley, I'd got a scholarship, and nothing had stood in the way.

Hold on. I was being expelled from Sweden, so how could I get this scholarship? I decided to call the person who had signed the letter and explained my situation. Her reply was the best gift that I ever heard. "You do not worry about that; we will fix it." Before I knew it, I received a letter from the immigration board requesting me to go and pick up my study and resident permit. For the first time in my life, my financial study woes were behind me because the Swedish Institute stipend is a generous one.

Early Life in Malawi and Going to Primary and Secondary School

I was born in 1963 in poor rural Malawi. I spent much of my early childhood experiencing first-hand what it was like to live without running water, electricity, and healthcare facilities while producing much of our own food needed for the family. Most vivid in my memories are the first two years of primary school education at Kailisi Primary School in Chisenga, Chitipa district. The school was not only far away. There were no chairs and no desks. The school only had a grass thatched roof and open spaces as windows. The school was two and a half English miles away. That is four kilometres, and by the time I reached school, I was not only hungry but also had difficulties concentrating. A hungry child is a difficult child, and I was often punished for not being attentive enough, making school very unattractive indeed. I was fortunate enough to have one saving grace, my grandmother, Lucy Nakayange. Every day when I came back from school, tired and hungry, my grandmother would have something special for me to eat, like groundnuts, and sometimes she surprised me with some eggs, *amafumbi*, from the chickens that we kept.

One day I decided that I had had enough of this thing called "school" and decided to skive off school. I left like I usually did, skipping to school, and then I hid in the bushes and made sure that everyone who was going to school had gone. If you look up Chisenga in Google Maps, it is still a remote area to this day. Many children simply did not have parents who could afford to pay the fees. On this particular day when I'd decided to miss school, I joined these children in playing and cooking sweet potato leaves in empty discarded tins. It was a wonderful day. It went by so quickly because soon, the other children started returning from school. I ran to meet them and asked if I could see their notebooks. I took out my pencil and copied down what they had done that day and, to make it more authentic, found a red pen to mark them and asked someone to write "very good". I skipped back home to Grandmother, who was always happy to see her grandchild.

My mother came back later from school, and after a while, she called me. Being a teacher in the school, she had found out that I had missed school that day, and she knew that I was not sick. To make sure that I would really understand how seriously to take education, for the following week in school, I was made to stand in the corner of the classroom of my mother. She had made her point that I would never forget. I often think that if I had received more of this type of punishment, I would have come to hate school.

Luckily for me, my dad got a job as a teacher in the city of Blantyre in southern Malawi, and the family moved from the impoverished village school to a better city school. What's more, I did not have to walk or run five kilometres to school each day. By now, my father was already at the time a well-travelled man and he knew and believed in the power of getting a good education as a tool to help one get out of poverty. Much to the disbelief of his male counterparts, he decided to invest heavily in sending me to some of the best primary and secondary schools in Malawi. It was quite amazing actually, given the size of his pay check. From the thatched roof of Kailisi primary school, I was sent to study standard two at Limbe Primary Private School. It was at about this time that my father went to attend a conference on "the gifted child" in Australia. He was himself presenting a paper, and when he came back to Malawi, he decided to transfer me to Our Lady's Convent in Limbe. I was quite unprepared for this move, and everything was happening so fast, Kailisi and now sitting in class with all these predominantly white and Asian children. Oh, by now, my father had a car, and I was driven to school back and forth. I have always been very curious and social and quickly made friends, but I could not help but notice that in the whole school, I think we were but a handful of black Malawian children. It was here that the nuns nurtured my passion for reading and the English language. When I first came to Our Lady's Convent, my English was not so good. One of the girls in my class used to tease me about that. *Huh,* I thought, *I am going to learn this language called English to the point that you will not recognise that it is not my native language.* I listened to the intonations, I practiced speaking, and most of all, I read and read.

Anytime we had to read out loud in class, I put my hand up to read, and when I was corrected, I simply ploughed on.

In 1973, my father's job saw us move from Blantyre to Zomba, and with that, I moved schools and started middle primary school at Sir Harry Johnston Primary School. Again, this was a predominantly Caucasian school with black Africans as a minority. It was here that I would see a swimming pool for the first time and watch how the white children could swim. If they could do it, so could I. The problem was that I did not have a swimming costume and so could not join the lessons. I asked my father if I could also have a swimming costume, and he simply said, "I have no money." This phrase, "I have no money," was a phrase that I would hear many times in my life. I longed to learn how to swim, but I dared not show that I did not have a swimming costume. Every now and then I would ask cautiously if I could have a swimming costume. Until one day, my father took me shopping for a swimming costume. It was the best day of my life; finally, I could also learn how to swim. I was so thrilled, and in earnest started to swim. Whenever the pool was open and we were allowed to swim, I would be in the water. So much did I like swimming that I won the school trophy in the breaststroke style. It made my father very proud, and I am sure he does not regret having bought that swimming costume. To this day, swimming remains my favourite sport.

But I was not always a calm and obedient student. While at Sir Harry Johnstone, I got into a lot of fights, mainly because someone would tease me about what I looked like. I decided the best way to defend myself would be to beat the kids. That way they would know better than to keep on taunting me. Of course, the parents and kids reported me to the headmaster. My father was asked to come to school to deal with this matter, thank God. This headmaster was extremely astute, and he realised that the problem was not that I was mean, but that I was frustrated. Instead of punishing me, he asked me if I would like to be a school prefect. Being a prefect meant that I could have a badge and be the one to tell the other students to behave. Of course, I would love to be a prefect! How smart of this headmaster. Now I would stop fighting, and the other children would have to listen to me as I was a school prefect. The responsibility that this position put on me was enough to lead me away from the path of self-destruction.

In 1975, I finished schooling at Sir Harry Johnston and had to change schools. This time, it was to be secondary school studies at St Andrews Secondary School in Blantyre. Since we lived in Zomba, it meant that I would have to attend the school as a boarder. I was very excited, especially because, although I was going to this "posh" English school, I was still expected to do quite a lot of the chores at home. When I got up, I would sweep the courtyard, mop the veranda and water and feed the chickens. When I got back from school, we would eat lunch, and I would have to help with taking care of my younger siblings. Sometimes all I wanted to do was just play with my friends, but I had to take care of my little siblings. The day I left for boarding school, I was very excited. Finally, I would be away from home, and I would not have to take care of my siblings or the chores that awaited me in the morning.

St Andrews was more mixed than Sir Harry Johnston, with children coming from other schools and countries. I met students from Zimbabwe, then called Rhodesia, Mauritius, Scotland, England, South Africa, Zambia, and more. It was here that I would meet the children of ministers for the first time. It was also at St Andrews that I was introduced to French and the trampoline, another sport that I quickly developed a love for. Alas, my time here was short-lived, as in 1976 my father was detained in prison, and my family could no longer afford to pay the school fees.

My mum and all of us were beside ourselves. On the morning when the heavily armed police men came to pick up my father, my father kept saying to my mother, "Irene, keep sending the children to school, no matter what happens." Even while in prison, my father surreptitiously sent messages to my mother to keep sending the children to school. My father asked my mother to ask a good friend to help her to get a transfer letter for me to attend a government secondary school. Due to lack of school fees, a dramatic move was made from St Andrews Secondary School to Nkhamenya Girls Secondary School in Kasungu where I spent two years studying form one and form two. This was a missionary school run by Canadian and Malawian nuns. What a change! I met girls from a variety of backgrounds from Malawi, but most of all we all worried about having enough money to pay the school fees. As girls, we also worried about having money to buy cotton wool for our monthly menstruation. The sisters being so aware of this problem would buy bulks of cotton wool and divide it into small, affordable portions for us to buy. To make it last longer, I would sometimes wrap toilet paper around so that the absorption would be better. At my poorest time in my life, I used rags of cloth that I would wash and reuse.

So it was not unusual that some of the girls in school had boyfriends who provided them with a bit of cash. Sometimes these were married men or much older men. The nuns were aware of some of these risks. Every term when we came back from holidays, we underwent a pregnancy examination. I lived in a dorm with fifteen other girls. One day, one of the girls was not feeling very well. She was feeling mostly nauseous and using her bucket for bathing to spit in. Normally, we would call the matron to come and look in on the sick girl, but this time, she asked not to have matron come. I remember thinking, *Oh, I do hope that she is not pregnant. Then she would be expelled from school.* Such was the case in my time of schooling. Unfortunately, it turned out to be true, and she had to leave school. I thought about her life and how it had changed with just that one event.

My life changed immensely once my father was imprisoned. He was released after four months with no compensation and remained unemployed for two years. During this period, the family relocated back to the village in Chisenga, and we became farmers once again. Back in poor rural Chisenga, observing my parents, particularly my Oxford-educated father relegated to the backwaters, I learned of the importance of networks and communication. You need to keep your networks alive. Every time I travelled back and forth to boarding school after the holidays, my father would give me the following messages: (1) "You are our ambassador. Do not do anything stupid," and (2) "I named you Linley after a female English professor because I know that girls can be talented," and (3) "School is the only thing that will get you out of this situation."

I managed to finish and pass the junior certificate graduation exam, and I was selected to go to Likuni Girls Secondary School in Lilongwe. My father, though very pleased, was very worried that going to continue my education in Lilongwe, the capital city, this would not be good for me. Too many dangers, he said. So he asked me to write a letter to the headmistress at Marymount Girls Secondary School in northern Malawi to see if I could transfer there instead. Fortunately, there was a student who wanted to transfer to Likuni, and so we switched places. Unlike Nkhamenya Girls, Marymount had a certain prestige around it, and the girls who came there already in form one seemed to feel like they owned the school. Then there was the division, those studying commerce and those studying domestic science. Since I came as a transfer student, I ended up joining the domestic science class. I was quite lucky because one of the teachers, a nun from Nkhamenya Girls, had also relocated to Marymount. This gave me much comfort. At Marymount, I managed to settle in, but I also had some challenges. Firstly, my years of schooling in the all-white schools would show me up – my English intonation was different. Secondly, in the domestic science classes, I knew quite a bit about some of the things that we had to cook. And later, my family was living in Ethiopia, and I would fly to Ethiopia to visit them. Sometimes when you stick out, things can work against you. In fact, the whole time I was studying at Marymount, I was assigned to the cleaning of the toilets. Until someone feeling pity for me asked if there were no other girls that could also do that task in the two years I was there. The harassment reached such a point that someone wrote a letter pretending to be signed by me to the headmistress complaining about things that I purportedly said. The headmistress, a very self-assured nun of African origin, was a wise woman, and she called for a general assembly meeting.

She never once mentioned my name, but she talked generally about false accusations, slander, and jealousy and how these hamper progress. I was so impressed by her ability to turn the situation around without making anyone personally feel singled out and how she managed to create a safe and enabling learning environment for many girls who may have felt as victims to some of the other students.

After two years of unemployment and living in the rural village of Chisenga, my father was reinstated as a lecturer at Chancellor College. I was now fifteen, slightly wiser and toughened by the experience of life in the village, travelling alone by bus and ever more curious and determined about schooling. Going to university in Malawi was not decided by the student, although one wrote the national examinations. One had to be selected. It became apparent that as a daughter of an academician from northern Malawi and former detainee, my chances of being selected were perhaps minimal. It was not long before my father took the bold decision to leave Malawi and fled with the family to Ethiopia. But it was not that easy for me to leave Malawi to join the family. Studying in a government secondary school, permission had to be sought from the Ministry of Education before leaving. My headmistress at Marymount Secondary made it possible for me to leave, never telling me that the government had rejected my application to leave the country.

Those Who Inspired Me in My Quest for Schooling

Much of my life has been influenced by schooling and the types of institutions running them. Throughout my primary and secondary school, I spent my life in boarding school in predominantly missionary schools. The nuns and brothers in these schools came from Ireland, England, Scotland, Canada, Malawi, and Zambia. While my father was imprisoned and unemployed, my mother was unable to pay the school fees, but I was never thrown out of school, especially while attending Nkhamenya Girls Secondary School when we literary had no money. The sisters simply ignored that fact, and one Catholic father made contributions whenever he could afford them. Nkhamenya Girls Secondary School remains very close to my heart with its motto, "More knowledge to serve better."

Travelling by bus from Chisenga to Nkhamenya Girls or to Marymount was not without risk – risk that the bus driver might over speed or fall asleep at the wheel and have an accident. To travel to Chitipa in those days, we needed to have a cholera vaccination certificate, and the bus United Transport of Malawi (UTM) passed through Zambia at Mulekatembo before driving back through Malawi. But the biggest risk was the possibility of young girls being coaxed into sleeping with the bus conductor. My brother Lekani knew this very well and he always tried to protect me when travelling together. So any time there was no bus and one had to hitch-hike, *matola*, as it is commonly known in Malawi, Lekani would always make sure that I looked dirty and wore a dress that was childish in nature, and we always sat next to each other speaking nothing but one of the many local languages that we both spoke fluently. But one time in 1977, I recall how I and another girl from the village, with our food packages, boarded the bus for Mzimba to return to school. Somewhere along Rhumpi, the bus broke down, and all the passengers had to make do with finding somewhere to spend the night. The mechanics had to come all the way from Mzimba, and one day went into two days, and the food we had brought with us slowly began to run out. With hardly any money, since my father was unemployed at the time, I knew that the situation was going to be precarious for us. Conductors always had money on them, and many girls would fall prey to their advances as a result of this. The second night, my friend had found transport for her and me on the back of a lorry. By now, schools had already started. The trip to Nkhamenya went fast, and somewhere in the night, we arrived at Nkhamenya turn-off. Since we did not have much luggage except a travelling bag, we alighted from the truck very quickly. The driver of the truck also got out, and taking the hand of the other girl who was much older than me, he said,

"I now need my payment that you promised." The payment, in this case, was not money but sex.

We panicked. My mother always insisted that when I travelled on public transport when going to school, I should always wear my school uniform so that if anything happened, people would recognise that I was a schoolgirl. I ran into the nearest bar that was open and shouted that my friend was being attacked. Upon seeing that there would be a problem, the driver let go of my friend, hurriedly reversed the truck, and hit the trunk of a Melina tree lining the road that junctions the Mzimba-Kasungu road and Nkhamenya Girls Secondary School. As long as that tree stood there, the mark that the truck left on that tree trunk became a constant reminder of the dangers that always lurked around for young girls travelling alone and in quest of education. The last time I saw the tree was in 2002.

Sometimes I had to be the main carer in the home, especially when my mother had to travel for weeks to visit my father in prison, and during this period, my grandmother was the one constant in my life, teaching me how to cook and farm. My mother was a stubborn woman, something that I found quite fascinating. She was a primary school teacher, always well-kept and dressed, no matter the occasion. She always had a side parting in her hair with a brooch pinned in her hair in the back. My mother shocked the village of Chisenga, pregnant and riding a bicycle in 1969 with me on the back carrier. When the family moved to Ethiopia, my mother learned how to drive and got the reputation of being one of the best cooks in Addis Ababa, especially with her signature scones, *matoke,* and ice-cream.

What most people did not know about this woman is how she very early in her life had to leave her first two children in Malawi when they were only two and four years old. Why? Because she travelled to England in 1966 to join her husband who was studying at Oxford University. While there, she worked as an auxiliary nurse. My parents were good friends of a well-established family in Oxford, and it was during this period that my mother learned so much about the British culture, something which she would embrace and employ in her own home to this day. This has greatly influenced my ways of being and thinking. The support from my mother to study further, though very harsh at times, has contributed significantly to my success.

The fact that my mother was a stay-at-home mum contributed to a stable home environment for the children. To this day, I wonder if I would have had half the tenacity that I put into pursing a higher education had I not been so provoked by one woman's statement in our home in Ethiopia. She said to my dad, "Linley, is she strong enough to do a PhD?" This woman had a PhD, and whenever she visited our home, she never once removed her plate from the table or went to the kitchen to help my mother to cook. *Surely*, I thought, *if this woman can have a PhD it cannot be that difficult.* To this day, I thank that woman for firing me up because she gave me the determination to endure and to prove her wrong.

I have often thought of how some men really promote women in their schooling and professions. I had two uncles who stood out in my life when it came to promoting girls' education in Malawi. My uncle Katoba Flax Musopole spoke English like he was born with it, and he had a degree in economics. His mantra to me was always, *"Mumanyilaghe isukulu* (make sure you get an education)," and he always talked about *"abandu aba bulu batamye leka* (uneducated people are difficult people)". I often thought, *How could he say that?* As years went by, I have come to realise that he meant well. The more schooling one has, the more one is able to question and comprehend things quickly. My journeys from the village to schools in more affluent situations have shown me that. Uncle Katoba also introduced me to the finer things in life way before I was to set foot in a country overseas. I remember when he first introduced me to a polony sandwich the equivalent of Italian mortadella. To this day, I will buy mortadella to remind myself of just how far I have come. Uncle Katoba was a self-proclaimed "unmarried" bachelor, and this was so unconventional in a country where marriage for a man of his calibre was the norm. The secret, he always said, was education and independence. Yes, this is so true. Living in a secularised country like Sweden, I see that the exposure my uncle gave me was way ahead of time.

And then there is that man in my life, the man who has stood by my side since we met during my early studies at Uppsala University, my husband, Erik. My foster mother, Rosa, put it very nicely while we sipped tea in the kitchen in Uppsala. "We shall never really know how you would have fared in Sweden had you been married to another man."

The choices that one makes in terms of a partner to share life with are very central to achieving one's goals. I came to Sweden to study beyond my wildest dreams, and the man I fell in love with has supported me tremendously with my ambitions to study. That would have to be another book the story of love and other things.

But what stands out most in my mentors is my father. At times, we had such a love-hate relationship, stubborn as mules, each one not wanting to give in to the other. My father was a worldly man. Realizing the dangers and temptations that a young girl, particularly a "broke" young girl, could be subjected to, my father ordered an extra American Express card for me to always be readily available while studying in the United States. He said, "Any time you are stranded and need to get out of a situation, use the card." It was unheard of in those days – the early eighties to be precise – that an "ordinary" African father would give his daughter an America Express credit card as a safety measure. This card helped quite a few girls of African origins while I was studying in the United States. To this day, I still keep the expired card with me.

Linley Chiwona-Karltun, PhD

(The American Express Card given to Linley by her father, Peter Chiwona, so she could always have a way out and depend on herself while studying in the United States for her undergraduate studies)

Migration to Sweden in Pursuit of Education

Driven by the opportunity to come and study without paying tuition fees, I, together with my father, bought a return plane ticket from Addis Ababa to Stockholm via London. After three months, if things did not work out, my father and I agreed that I would return to Addis to continue with my quest for sourcing funds to complete my master's degree at Tulane School of Public Health and Medicine. I arrived at Arlanda in Sweden on 12 March 1988, a year that proved to be one of the coldest winters in decades. I had been told that Sweden was expensive, but I had not quite understood just how expensive it really was. Without the kindness of so many people, life would have been unbearable, especially from loneliness. Despite having gone to school in the UK and United States, nothing had quite prepared me for living in Sweden. When I was running low on food or at times without food, I had some dear friends who saw to it that I shared the little they had. We ate the cheapest sources of food, like chicken hearts and gizzards or old retired chickens, *höns*. One time, I was so broke that I called my father to please help me out because I could see no way out. I vividly recall receiving a check for five hundred US dollars that only translated into SEK2500. *How*, I wondered, *would I pay for my rent and live off this money?* This was before I had the resident permit to work. Without the generous support of the people and friends whom I had made good relations with, it would have been difficult for me to survive in Sweden. At the same time, I knew that this sacrifice from my father was probably all the money that he could spare for a very long while. I still recall reading the letter from my father that came with this check written in May 1988.

The letters from Dad were never long, and they always ended with "love, Dad." Though I never really pondered over the significance of those last two words in my younger days, with time, those words became very powerful symbols. "You are our ambassador." My dad said those very same words when he sent me off to school in the United States in 1983: "Remember: you are our ambassador." I remember telling my room-mate in the United States in the dorm when I was first received at ECU that my father said I had to behave as if I was an ambassador. I will never forget the look on her face. She did not understand this, and she found it to be quite funny. I asked if she really knew the meaning of the word *ambassador* because for me, I felt so proud when my father said I was their ambassador. To this day, I still feel that I am an ambassador for Malawi. My father never said, "Behave yourself," and perhaps by not saying it like that, he lowered the pressure on behaving well. Instead, I simply felt very privileged to be an ambassador from Malawi.

Without the kindness of the people who I met in my early days in Sweden guiding me carefully through the Swedish system and teaching me how to survive with the smallest of means, life would have been infinitely more difficult for me. In those days, exotic food, like dried kidney beans or basmati rice, were not very common place, and knowing where to find them as a foreigner was difficult unless someone knew these places. The Swedish language made things substantially more challenging, and I quickly realised that to survive in Sweden, even if it was for a short while, learning the language was important. One of the administrators at the department where I was doing my studies assisted me in enrolling for Swedish classes. Though relatively easy to get by with English in Sweden, I made it a point to start practicing speaking Swedish, reading newspapers as well as listening to the Swedish radio, especially P1. Watching English television programmes with Swedish subtitles proved invaluable in seeing how words were spelt and what words were in Swedish. Having moved so much in my younger days, I understood the value of knowing and speaking the local language. Furthermore, having seen my father struggle, I knew that ably speaking the Swedish language would be fundamental to my success.

Though fully trained as a dietician in the United States, it was not possible for me to work as a dietician in Sweden. First, I was required to get my education evaluated by the Swedish Higher Education Authority (UHÄ). This took eighteen months of patience. When I eventually received the evaluation, it showed that the professional degree from the United States was one semester longer than the Swedish degree. Still that did not enable me to work as a dietician, as I was told, the language, foods, and diet in Sweden differed significantly, and I needed to learn these things. Undeterred, I signed up for courses that would give me the skills in "*Svensk måltidsplanering and Svensk Matlagning*". With my passion for cooking and very early training in domestic sciences and cookery, plus the skills inherited from my grandmother and mother, combined with my mother-in-law Ingrid Karltuns' expert guidance into Swedish society, I had a natural flare for the courses. One day the teacher brought a basket full of different mushrooms and started to ask the class one by one if we knew the names. Apart from me, everyone in the class was what you would call an "indigenous Swede", studying to become a dietician. Surprisingly, none of the students could identify any of the mushrooms except me. Equipped with these courses plus my degree from the United States, I thought I might get a job as a dietician. I joined the union for the dieticians, and I went to the annual Nordic meeting for dieticians in Norway. In the end, the closest I ever came to working as a dietician in Sweden was working as a *köksbiträde*, kitchen aide, in the dietician's kitchen, preparing breast milk for premature babies. Had I come all the way to Sweden to take on the job of the equivalent of a scullery maid in the hospital? Imagine what my parents would say to their friends. If anything at all, working as a scullery maid really propelled my Swedish skills as most of the people I worked with did not speak English or simply felt uneasy speaking English. As I walked the corridors of the hospital, delivering the bottles of breast milk to the wards, I noted how invisible I was. How was it possible to be present and yet not be present at the same time?

Getting Professional Academic Qualifications in Sweden

Ethiopia remains the central point and dot connector of my origins, passion, career, and scientific engagement. I realised rather early that it was important for me to go back to Africa while doing my bachelor's degree in the United States. The thing that pulled me back to Africa so strongly was the famine in Ethiopia during 1984–5. *Why,* I had wondered, *and how could it be that my family lived in Ethiopia, and yet I had not seen this mass starvation being displayed on television in the United States?* The word "why" would come up time and again, sometimes together with "how". The famine in Ethiopia was the first point of entry, so much pain and so unnecessary. My chance meeting with scientists in the area of poverty and nutrition from 1987 contributed to my building up a scientific portfolio as a researcher. My first output was an annotated bibliography on coping with famine in Ethiopia. The second fortuitous meeting was with an expert on iodine-deficiency disorders. Having explained my interest to learn more about hunger and poverty, I was given a signed copy of the book *The Story of Iodine Deficiency: An International Challenge in Nutrition.* This signed book was to prove most useful when looking for opportunities to further my studies.

When I came to Sweden, I took these documents plus the CV, and whenever the opportunity arose, I showed them to people I judged as being able to listen to my query for pursuing my education. Unbeknown to me, iodine research was being pursued by some scientists at Uppsala University, and I was asked to write a concept paper on iodine deficiency and to submit it to the professor.

I spent days working on this and asked my first Swedish friend, Amal, to read it first. I will never forget the first comment that Amal asked me: "All these words that you are using, do you know their meanings?"

I answered truthfully. "Not all of them."

"Well then," said Amal, "then you better make sure you do in case you are asked to explain." That was my first lesson: read, understand, and know what you are saying, inside out.

When I handed in the draft paper to Professor Mehari Gebre-Medhin, the first comment was, "You really seem to have read a lot about the area. Tell me where and how you found the information." I was so glad my friend had prepared me well.

The second thing he pointed out was my style of writing. "Linley," he said, "this is not a Shakespeare literary writing event – keep to the facts, and keep it short." Scientific writing, especially in the medical sciences, uses as few words as possible.

Through Professor Mehari's mentorship and guidance, I avoided falling between the cracks as an immigrant in Sweden. So many times, Professor Mehari would tell me, "If you spend your time mingling in the underground clubs of Stockholm, you will not make it in Sweden. Linley, from my experience, Sweden is a very good place for a girl like you, but you need to work hard and most of all you need to be loyal with those you work with and, in turn, they will be loyal to you."

In fact, without Mehari's guidance, it may never have been possible for me to study and move within an academic environment. It would not be too far-fetched to say that without Professor Mehari, or MGM, as we used to call him, my stay and life in Sweden may have been short-lived.

When I commenced my studies in the Swedish university system, I continued to think that I had to wait to be spoken to before speaking and that I could not be too critical. For so long, I had been conditioned to think that being too critical would result in some sort of reprisal. One day, I was attending a course, and one professor was teaching about cassava and how the people eating cassava had been poisoned by it somewhere in Mozambique. My palms were sweaty; my heart was racing with anger more than anything else. Growing up with my grandmother in the village in Chisenga, we had grown cassava, eaten cassava fresh and as a starchy porridge, and nothing had happened. What on earth was he talking about? Typical *mzungu*, white people. I raised my hand and said that cannot be true because in my village cassava was not dangerous. After class, we had a long discussion about cassava in Malawi, and as the saying goes, the rest is history. That conversation was to be the start of my long trip of my PhD training. Hans Rosling, now ordained Chief Tauno in Liberia for his contributions in the Ebola fight, was passionate about cassava and understanding poverty, particularly when it came to Africa. Under the guidance of Hans Rosling, I was to learn of how important it was to speak with facts and figures before making any claims.

My doctoral training was one of the most interesting and most convoluted periods of my schooling. Why did farmers prefer to use bitter and toxic cassava? That was the thesis of my doctoral studies. To answer this question, I had to carry out a lot of field surveys, some experiments, and some more interpretation of the interviews that I carried out with the farmers.

I started off with one child, Karin, and in the process had another child, Nora. The biological clock does not wait for a woman to complete her studies, so I combined childbearing, motherhood, and education. Things did not always work out well. Stress, migraine, and painkillers became common features of my life during this period. Fortunately for me, I was referred for further examination at the neurology ward where it was determined that my migraine was triggered by my work and lifestyle. With this prognosis, I slowed down, reduced my ambitions, and took my time to complete my studies. After all, the only person I was competing with was myself.

Presenting your findings in an international conference is instrumental in letting your peers know about whom you are and what your research is about. I submitted my abstract which was selected for an oral presentation. Having been to only a couple of conferences, I felt honoured and a little apprehensive. In those days, PowerPoint was just beginning to take centre stage, so PowerPoint it was. The day came to make the presentation, and I took to the stage to present, nervous as hell. My supervisor had prepared me extremely well, content-wise. After all, he is world renowned for that. I was filled with doubt, especially when I saw the auditorium mostly filled with men. It brought back feelings of being alone, travelling to secondary school in rural Malawi. Then I remembered my time at Marymount Secondary School and my drama club. I remembered my English teacher coaching me for my role as Odede's mother in our award-winning play and how I had won the prize for best diction. All I needed to do was to play my role in this play and tell the audience what the farmers were telling about why they preferred bitter cassava. It was probably the best presentation of my life. After the presentation, my team from the field that also attended the conference were full of congratulations. But this feeling of euphoria did not last for long. It turned out that while the presentation was good, there was some doubt about whether I really had been out in the field and done the fieldwork by myself.

(Linley visiting a flourishing cassava field in Thailand in 2002, an experience she carried over to her cassava research and development studies with cassava farmers in Malawi. Photo: Opas Boonseng)

How could this thought begin to cross someone's mind? Sure, I had worked with field assistants, but since I could speak the local languages, I conducted the interviews with their support. I was to learn that science is a much-contested hierarchical field. Who did I think I was, coming there, a young girl based in Sweden speaking with some "funny English accent"? Being my first-ever international conference, I was crushed and stressed out, inducing a migraine onset. The support from my well-experienced supervisor was immeasurable. I was to learn that it is not unusual that scientific results are contested by different schools of thought. I was to learn that while some of my science could be easily referred to by some scholars, some schools of thought would never consider referring to. I was to learn much later that even in science, there is a gender preference for men to quote and to elevate each other's works more than those of women. As a young doctoral student, I simply thought that science was science, and little did I know that in science, nepotism and sexism abound as illustrated by research findings.

My doctoral training years gave me the opportunity to experience and to learn many things about myself and others. I remember embarking on the writing of my first manuscript for publication. I was to put together my findings from my qualitative interviews with farmers in the field from Malawi. It was the most difficult thing. The results were there, but how on earth do you write a scientific paper? I wrote the first version, then the second, third, fourth, and on and on. My supervisor, a stickler for perfection, kept asking me to elaborate more. *How?* I would ask.

He said, "Go back to the data, the interviews, the tapes, and listen again. What exactly are the farmers saying in their language? Listen to each word." I swear, by the time I reached the tenth version, I was ready to give up the damn PhD studies. *What was so difficult to understand from my writing?*

My supervisor, seeing my frustration, decided on a strategy that would to this day influence how I work with my students. "Send me a page at a time as soon as you finish." Every time I sent him a page, he would give me feedback. By now email was catching on, so communication was much more fluid. It took us up to eighteen versions of the manuscript, prior to submission. When I was given the go-ahead to finally submit to the journal, I was delighted. The outcome was that the manuscript was accepted with minor revisions. To this day, it remains my most-treasured publication because I had been through the arduous task and knew just how hard it was to write a good manuscript. By the time I was writing my final manuscript for the thesis, I was more mentally prepared for the long process of writing, rewriting, and waiting to eventually get a manuscript published. Still, every time a rejection decision comes, it is just as painful today.

Finally, the big day came when I concluded my doctoral studies. What a joy for both me and my father, who came all the way from Malawi to Sweden to witness the public defence. My dad came together with my "little brother" Pierre, ever a staunch supporter of my success and a dedicated baby-sitter of my daughters Karin and Nora.

Pursuing a Career in the Scientific Academy

Teaching in academic environments with a research base proved to be extremely useful. I could use my ongoing research findings as case studies for understanding deeper issues of food security, poverty, and rural development. While working as an adjunct lecturer, together with a multidisciplinary group of colleagues, we established the first Global NutITion programme that brought together professionals working with agriculture, nutrition, and health in 1999 to use information technology tools to update their skills and knowledge. The aim of this programme was for the participants to create networks and their own geographically relevant teaching materials. The programme ran for six years with participants from Africa, Asia and Latin America and established a strong network of over 150 professionals who, to this day, keep in touch in one way or another. Professionally, this network has provided substantive networking support for me.

Being of African origin in a country like Sweden, your colour clearly stands out amidst the crowd, and there are very few professionals of African or black origins in the academic sphere. While issues of gender equality are visibly brought to the forefront in terms of employment and promotion, rarely are issues of colour or diversity discussed. As time went by, I felt the need to interact and connect with other women of colour or similar backgrounds to discuss "our issues". Not finding anything already in existence, a group of African women scientists came together and formed a network of academic African women in Sweden. This group of women has proven to be a great pillar of support and led to the establishment of the Network of African European Women Scientists (NAWES) in Sweden.

Very often I have been confronted with the question: how does a minority find a platform or voice for his or her contributions? It seems much easier to do that outside of Sweden, especially if one is pursuing science, as science knows no boundaries. Good science is good science. After twenty-eight years and having lived more than half of my life in Sweden, I had to acknowledge that I was by now a full-fledged African in the Diaspora. Whether I like it or not, I will always be connected to Africa or to all things African by virtue of my colour and biological origins, and these attributes will at times be used to judge me or to form opinions. That is not bad in itself, as it has given me a force to be engaged using my science as a basis for discussion and entry into society as a whole.

As an African in the Diaspora, I have found that one always has to be a hustler, and finding like-minded people with similar experiences became key to moving my scientific and social agenda ahead. After years of being an African minority in academia in Sweden, I had noticed a particular trend. While studying in the United States, I noted that graduates of any particular university would identify themselves not only with paraphernalia from the school but also with reunions of various sorts. It struck me as odd that the universities in Sweden at the time of my studies did not have such a well-established alumni culture, especially for international students. In addition, most of the communication language was Swedish, meaning that most former students did not even understand the communication that they received from their universities. I wanted to give recognition to the many African students who had studied at one of the institutions where I worked. Most of the graduates had progressed to become well-accomplished professionals around the world. In 2010, I was invited to an International Conference for Higher Education in Agriculture (CHEA) hosted by the Regional Universities Forum for Agriculture (RUFORUM) in Uganda. With backing from Professor Stella Williams, I received support from the vice chancellor of the Swedish University of Agricultural Sciences (SLU) to co-host the first-ever SLU-Africa Alumni side event, titled "Africa in SLU and SLU in Africa". This side event was supported by the Association of African Agricultural Professionals in the Diaspora (AAAPD) United States, and paved way for the European chapter,

AAAPD-Europe, of which I am the president. I continue to strive for the visibility and affirmation of people of African descent within the academic sphere in Sweden, not least at my current place of work.

Retaining networks is a challenging task which painstakingly requires skills and management. The longer the relationships are maintained and the more frequent the contact and, particularly, joint activities, whether social or professional, the greater the impact on my professional success. This story of networking would be half an unfinished story if a chance meeting with Dr Lindiwe Sibanda had not taken place. One can attribute much to chance, but chance alone without a prepared active mind does not amount to much. Lindiwe was introduced to me through a common acquaintance when I was looking for a resource person to conduct training on communicating agricultural policy and development. At the time, I was working for the International Foundation for Science (IFS) as a scientific programme coordinator and trainer in scientific communication. Lindiwe was a fine communicator and mentor and, most importantly, a wonderful role model for me ever since our serendipitous meeting. There are very few accomplished African women who take it upon themselves to mentor and open doors for other women. Let us celebrate more publicly those who do these things. As I have reached a point in my career to pay it forward, I take pride when, in some of my training or supervisory roles, I hear a participant or student say, "I want to be just like Linley." My response is, "You can be better than Linley."

At times, I have merely been thinking about surviving in the system, grasping at many different tasks. Multitasking sooner or later takes a toll on you. If one wants to pursue a life in science or academics, the earlier one finds out what the criteria for promotion and success are, the better. But that alone is not enough. One needs people that can not only mentor and coach you but also sponsor you. By "sponsor", I mean people who will mention your name in the right circles, lend your name as credible, and indicate that you are worth investing in. Without sponsors, I have found that climbing up the ladder, getting that much needed position, or even accessing relevant information for funding opportunities is difficult. Being a person of African origin and black colour – add "woman" on top – is a combination rife with challenges. It is important not to become bitter or to despair when things seem so futile. Reassess, strategize, and rally support from your trusted network. Most importantly, get affirmed; when you are affirmed by your rallying network, you will rise up again.

So, Does Education Matter?

More than one can imagine. Because education equips you with unimaginable tools. One day in 2015 I received a message from my sister Linda in the United States. "Linley, your friend Alison is looking for you. There will be a school reunion, and she wonders if you can make it." Thirty-four years had gone by since I had last seen Alison. My best friend from boarding school, Our Lady's Convent High School in Alnwick, Northumberland, had found me once again. Just the thought of meeting all my friends from school led to memories of the cafeteria and apple turnovers that made my mouth water. It is impossible to describe the feelings and memories that the reunion brought out. But one thing stands out: meeting the domestic science teacher again was a dream come true. She was the first domestic science teacher to instil in me the desire to be professional in cookery. The basic science foundations for understanding how to prepare, refresh, preserve, and cook things I had mastered while studying under her tutelage. When I applied for university studies, I knew that it had to be something with food and management and, hence, my first degree in food nutrition and institutional management. To this day, my pastries are never soggy, my cakes as fluffy as can be, and my roast turkey as succulent as it should be. What's more, the principles of cookery are the same, and all I needed to do was adapt to the context and the food. Thirty-four years later, I had the opportunity to thank her for making cookery science such an interesting class. Cookery brought me closer to my brother Andy, currently a brilliant chef, changed my life, and influenced my professional career. Every year on my birthday I celebrate my cookery skills with my signature dish, "Linley's beans and rice".

Without education, this story would not have been told, at least not as it is. I have learnt and experienced very early that as a girl, and later as a woman, if you are illiterate and poor, you really have some hurdles to overcome compared to a girl or woman who is literate. Moving around the world, I also found out that this position is further compounded if I am of black and African origins. When I find myself in a public meeting and I dare to speak or question something, I need to be spot on. Too much rambling on, not being succinct enough or articulate in my speech, simply paves the way for dismissal and confirmation of the "backwardness" or lowliness" of blacks or Africans.

My experience has shown that a strong command of spoken and written language, in-depth knowledge of the subject matter, excellent up-to-date knowledge of current and world events will enable you to command respect. When as a woman you take centre stage and when you superimpose black colour onto that podium, you need to leave an indelible mark, never to be forgotten. It becomes the world, a stage, and you an actor making the performance of your life. You need to pitch it right with the voice, time it right with the allocated time, and use the visual aids with precision and appropriateness. To cap it all, you need to be dressed for the part: ask a friend, a colleague, your children, or your family to give you some honest feedback before leaving home. Because when your cherished ones say you look good, that is half the battle won for that day.

Nowhere did the combination of these skills prove to be as useful as when raising my children Karin and Nora or when interacting with the welfare and social services in Sweden. A good command of the Swedish language combined with my attainment of higher education has enabled me to fight for the rights of my African-Swedish children when attending parent-teacher meetings or even getting them to be a part of some extracurricular social activities. But it also made it possible for me to speak up for the other minority parents who, due to their challenges with the language, were unable to express themselves. For my children, knowing that their African-Swedish mother is learned has provided them with a platform and positive learning environment to excel in life. I truly believe that with children living in a country where their colour represents a minority group, higher education attainment of their parents is a crucial determinant of their own success.

From Chisenga, Chitipa, to Ethiopia, to Northumberland - England, to North Carolina - USA, to Ethiopia, to Sweden and the world beyond, I bear with me an enormous wealth of knowledge and experience that simply cannot be discounted professionally. Unstoppable. I often tell people that pursuing studies in cassava has made me so wealthy in terms of experience, friends, and career, and cassava has also made me globally savvy. Now, seriously, who would have thought that soaking cassava in *ingumbe* (earthernware pots) in Chisenga with my grandmother would one day lead me to studying cassava and making a career out of it? I share my story with you and hope that you will be inspired and trust that you will gather the courage to aspire to pursue higher education. Quitting never allows you to win.

Pauline Ocaya, PhD

Aim High and Challenge Yourself

"Education is the most powerful weapon which you can use to change the world." Nelson Mandela

Pauline Ocaya, PhD

Acknowledgments

Much has happened, and I am sure more is to come.

I wish to thank you who have been part of my journey this far, who have in one way or another encouraged and inspired me, who have shared the ups and downs of life with me.

Thank you, Mats, for your input during the writing of this chapter.

Last but not least, I wish to thank my parents, sisters, and brothers for their love and support.

One warm afternoon in July 2014, I was at a laboratory, sitting on a swivel chair next to a physician who had specialized in microbiology and infectious diseases. I was sitting next to this person who had not only one area of expertise but also was specialized in two medical fields. The setting was the microbiology laboratory at Karolinska University hospital, a hospital that is recognized internationally for its medical research and health care. I was a medical student working as a laboratory engineer during my summer vacation. The doctor and I were analysing samples from patients trying to identify the properties of microorganisms that could be causing their symptoms. Deeply concentrating, with our eyes on diagnostic plates containing bacteria colonies, we were determining whether the specific strain was sensitive or resistant to a set of antibiotics. The doctor measured a clear zone around an antibiotic disc and told me, "Different cut-off values are used to determine the sensitivity to different antibiotics. If the bacteria is resistant to an antibiotic currently used to treat the patient, the treating physician has to re-evaluate the choice of treatment based on our analysis."

I was sitting there, nodding, taking notes, asking questions, and remembering lectures I'd had a few months earlier and at the same time thinking about the lives that potentially were being saved by the analysis performed at the laboratory. I could feel the excitement growing inside me even more than when I first joined medical school, the excitement of knowing that I was on a path leading to a place where I could help people in need.

Early Life and Education

I was born in 1980 in northern Uganda, and I am the oldest of four siblings and several step siblings. My father was away working when my mother went into labour with me, so my uncle took my mother to the nearest bus stop on his bicycle. Well there, afraid that my mother would deliver on the bus, the bus driver did not want to let her on. He eventually allowed her to get on, but on the condition that she sat on the floor during the entire 5-kilometre ride.

After a few years in northern Uganda, the family relocated to Kampala, where my father was working. There I joined preschool and later enrolled in primary school. My father is a civil engineer and a strong advocate for education. At a time and place when not everyone saw the value in educating girls, my father would say, "No daughter of mine is going to be left without an education." So from an early age, my father talked to me about the power and importance of education. However, soon after starting primary school, my dear father had to exile to Kenya due to political instability in Uganda. My father left Uganda as political refugee after the military overthrew the government and was arresting those who supported it. As the persecutors were looking for him with the belief that we were hiding him, we became more isolated, and my sister and I had to stop going to school and preschool respectively. When the political climate became a little better, my father made arrangements for us to move to Kenya.

When my father first came to Kenya, he started working for a German construction company. He had built a house for his family in the neighbourhood where his German colleagues lived. We adjusted to our new life in Kenya, and my sister and I returned to school. I was fluent in my mother-tongue, Acholi, and was also able to communicate in English since it was the official language in Uganda. It was also the language my father used when talking to us kids. In Kenya, I had to learn Swahili, which was the language primarily spoken when not in the classroom. Being able to speak English worked to my advantage, as it was the language spoken in the classrooms and whenever a teacher was present. I learned Swahili with ease without thinking about the fact that I was learning a new language.

The family seemed to settle well in the new place. However, it turned out that the Kenyan colleagues at the company did not approve of our living arrangements, where my father had chosen to live in the same neighbourhood as his German co-workers. This caused turbulence at his workplace and resulted in the relocation of the family. Apparently, the colleagues had been unsatisfied with the situation for a while, and my father, aware of this, had started building another home for us. The new place was beautiful and in a remote area close to nature. As we were getting adjusted to the move and getting back to our daily routines, we suddenly had to move again. The colleagues were not happy with that solution either. Thus, we packed and moved to a different city.

The first months in the new city were spent living in an apartment belonging to a local businessman who my father got in touch with before moving from the previous city. My father got a small plot and, once again, began building a home for his family. He built four apartments in a block, and we moved in. As the apartments were being built, my sister and I joined a Christian primary school where some teachers were Catholic nuns. Having easily overcome the language barrier, I could now make friends with great ease. The family grew in number, and from my perspective, life was once again back to being normal with the daily routines in place. However, little did I know, things were about to change again. Despite his qualifications, bureaucracy and, probably to a great extent, discrimination made it difficult for my father to get a proper employment. My father left his family to try and find a better future and opportunity for us. Time went by, and every now and then my mother and stepmother received news that my father was okay. Eventually, they found out that he had made his way to Sweden and was making arrangements for my sisters, stepmother, and step siblings to travel there. My mother, brother, and I were to travel at a later stage.

For us who remained, life changed in the apartment complex as a physician set up a private practice in one of the apartments. He was an extremely kind and knowledgeable physician, which was evident by the fact that the number of patients visiting his practice grew steadily for each day. It did not take long after opening the practice before the waiting room was too small to hold his patients. Patients would sit on the veranda, extending almost all the way to our apartment. I saw patients who looked extremely sick who, during their return visits, seemed to have recovered from whatever was making them ill. I found this amazing and could not help wondering, *How did he make them better? What did he do?* My brother suffered from childhood spastic attacks and the close proximity to a good physician meant that he was able to receive proper health care when needed. I always worried about my brother and had become used to the helplessness I felt whenever he had an attack. *Why is this happening? Will he be all right? What can I do?* These were some of the questions I had asked myself over and over. And I could see the same questions written on my mother's face.

Growing up with my brother's condition and having patients around me awoke my curiosity about the human body. *How did the human body work? Why do some people become ill and not others? How are people cured? What exactly does their medication do?* My brother's condition made me wonder why some diseases could be cured while others kept on coming back. As he became older, his attacks became less frequent and later disappeared, which only made me more curious. *I want to understand what is happening to my brother.* This frustration and my father's words about the power of education encouraged me to study hard, thinking, *I may be able to understand as long as I study.*

Seeing that patients every now and then would need something to eat, my mother set up a small business. It provided drinks, fruits, and some to-go food and was highly appreciated by the patients. This made me learn the importance of identifying and grabbing opportunities. I admired how my mother had identified the opportunity and decided to do something about it. My mother had quickly calculated risks versus benefits and made her move. But underneath it all, the will to help others was what had motivated her the most. As years passed by, my dear mother and uncle thought that I had become too mischievous and decided to send me to live with Catholic nuns at a nearby Catholic monastery.

At the monastery, I found four other girls living there either on the same basis as myself or due to poverty. Living there meant taking care of chores and being on top of your schoolwork, which meant the girls and I had to be extremely disciplined to cope. The daily agenda entailed waking up hours before school, taking care of chores which included cleaning the entire premises, preparing breakfast and lunch for the nuns, planning for dinner, taking care of the domestic animals, having a quick breakfast, and making it to school before 7.00 a.m. School ended at 17.00 p.m., and we hurried back to our evening chores, evening mass, and tending to our homework before getting to bed. I got a long with the other girls and ended up liking the discipline that came along with living at the monastery. Of course, I missed my mother and brother, but I had quickly gotten used to the hard work, the quick pace, and the new environment. Not long after moving to the monastery, my aunt became ill, and my mother went to Uganda to take care of her. Around that time, my stepmother came for my brother and me, and we moved to Sweden.

Source of Inspiration when Growing Up

From an early age, my father instilled in me the importance of education. He would speak of education as if it was the only key to a happy life, as if the world was made of doors and education was a magical key that could unlock all of those doors. I remember him occasionally opposing my mother when she wanted me to do chores. "Let her do her homework," he would say. He continued talking about education even as I became older. "Study hard and make a future for yourself, Pauline," he would say. "Make sure you have qualifications because you will realize that life is tough. However, it is much tougher if you do not have an education. I am telling you this for your own sake. Your younger siblings will all be hearing the exact words that I am saying to you."

My father has gone through a lot of hardships, but his passion for education never declined. This "un-declining" passion would inspire the most uninspired person. I am sure my father will be telling his grandchildren, Isac and Alice, only to name few, the exact same things he once told me. He has always moved forward, regardless of what was placed in front of him, always trying to find a way for what he believed. Not that I always knew what was going on in his head. Nor could I understand all of his decisions and choices. However, when it came to education, his belief that everyone should have the right to it regardless of sex, meant that my siblings and I could easily access that world. I will always be grateful for the inspiration and support.

One of my greatest and most important sources of inspiration has been, continues to be, and will always be my dear mother. I have fragments of memories from when we were still living in northern Uganda before relocating to Kampala. I was only a few years old and was being carried on my mother's back. My mother had gone to the river to fetch water in a bucket that was now balancing steadily on her head. On our way back, we went to a market where she bought some items. So she was walking there, singing, with a baby on her back, a bucket of water balancing on her head, and groceries in her hands.

I was brought up by a strong, hardworking, and kind woman who, by merely being there, inspired me to work hard and set goals for the future. Her strength assured me that I could become whatever I wanted and that I must not accept being looked down on because of my sex. Those who do not know my mother may from the looks of her think of her as extremely fragile. But looks do deceive in this case. Having to let go of her children without knowing when she would be reunited with them again takes courage and strength. She always looked ahead, solving one obstacle at a time. Even when the odds did not seem to favour her, she kept on working hard. This taught me not to give up at the first sight of an obstacle. Seeing how my mother tackled problems of all sizes and found ways to overcome them made me realize that giving up was taking the easy way out. It takes more strength, courage, and skills to rise above an obstacle. The way my mother kept on moving was kind of a statement made saying, "Giving up is not an option." Her actions spoke louder than words, and it has always been enough to get inspired just to watch her.

The physician who set up a private practice next door to our apartment in Kenya was a great source of inspiration. He came in early in the morning, worked hard, and left late. Many people arrived at his practice suffering from different conditions. I would at times catch him expressing concerns about his patients to the nurse. He seemed to really care about his patients and wanted the well-being of everyone seeking his help. When severely sick patients arrived at his practice, I would find myself wondering whether the doctor would be able to help them. When they came back for their check-ups, most of them looked as if they were feeling better, whereas a few did not. *What made one drug superior over another? Why did some get better while others did not? What was the difference?* I got curious about what happened to the human body in the state of a disease and how drugs worked in order to make people get better. The way the practitioner from the very start seemed to know what to do when my brother had his attacks made me think, *I too would like to help people the way he does. I would like to have enough knowledge to do something, and not just be a helpless bystander.* Thus, one of my greatest motivations to study hard was primarily my brother, or more specifically, his childhood illness. The physician, being someone with enough knowledge to help my brother, inspired me immensely.

In high school, I had a chemistry and biology teacher who had a way of teaching that made these subjects vibrant. This drove me to dive into these subjects and get the foundation required for my later studies. During my last year of high school, I could not keep my eyes out of human pathology books. I would sit during breaks, flipping through the pages, telling my classmates about different diseases. This great interest was probably because of what I had seen growing up. The fact that my teacher inspired me to take on biology and chemistry gave me the knowledge and a starting point to enter the world of human physiology and pathophysiology.

Being the oldest of many siblings, I would always hear my parents and close friends to the family saying, "Your younger siblings will follow your footsteps, so you have to show them the way. If you succeed, then the probability of them succeeding is also greater." This felt unfair. Why should all the responsibility be placed on me? What they were saying translated in my head into, *Make sure you do not fail; if you do and your siblings ever fail, it will all be your fault.* Somehow I turned the pressure into something positive and eventually, the more I heard this, the more it pushed me to do my best. I was working hard for my future and if the pressure put on me could help me reach my goal, then so be it. Moreover, if working hard would be helping my siblings along the way, then that was just great.

Migration to Sweden and First Years

When I arrived in Sweden, I was twelve years old, soon turning thirteen. Even though excited about seeing my siblings and father again, I was saddened by the fact that my mother was not with me. It had been years since I had last seen my siblings, which made me nervous. I started wondering, *Are my siblings going to remember me? Are they the same people I remember, or have they changed a lot? Is it going to feel like meeting strangers? What about my brother, having to leave his mother at the age of five and move to a new country to a father he did not know?*

To some extent, seeing my father and siblings felt like meeting with strangers. They were all communicating with such ease in a language totally incomprehensible to me. My siblings by now seemed so in place in Sweden, a country new to my brother and me. Moreover, I quickly realized that I could not spend time reminiscing about our lives in

Kenya. My siblings had already forgotten a lot. This created a sense of distance between us, which made me miss my friends and the daily life I had left behind.

I arrived in Sweden in summer and enrolled in school that autumn. I spent the first semester learning Swedish together with other classmates who were also from other countries. Many of the classmates came from countries where the Arabic language was spoken and could, therefore, find a connection through that. Seeing that there was no one from an English-speaking country in the class, I first felt that I was without luck. However, since groups that could speak another language tended to use it instead of Swedish, it became a barrier making it more difficult for them to advance in Swedish. I was, however, forced to use Swedish at all times, which allowed me to advance faster. Since Swedish was the only language allowed amongst pupils in the classroom, everyone was forced to try his or her best. The fact that everyone was a beginner made it easier to learn through trial and error, which created a positive learning environment. Moreover, since I already spoke English, I was able to communicate easily with my teacher when necessary. I was grateful, as I could see how difficult it was for the other pupils to make themselves understood when talking to the teacher.

In order to make progress, I worked hard on my assignments and would, whenever possible, try to take part/initiate conversations in Swedish with my siblings. Seeing that the conversation pace slowed down whenever I participated, I worked even more on what I had pinned down as my weakness: pronunciation and the speech melody. I watched Swedish news channels and constantly bothered my siblings in order to get the pronunciation correct. To increase my vocabulary, I read children's books and concentrated on understanding the Swedish subtitles when watching American/British programmes on TV. One of the hardest things was not letting frustration take over. I decided not to care if people laughed at my pronunciation, and that I would not take the easy way out which would have been to speak Swedish only when in class. After one semester in that class, the teachers assessed my Swedish to be good enough. Thus, I joined a regular class with Swedish natives and pupils who were fluent in Swedish. Apart from English, all other subjects were held in Swedish. I worked hard and passed all the subjects required for high school.

Before preparing my applications for high school, I spoke to my father, revealing that I wanted to become a pilot. He advised me to reconsider and that becoming a nurse may be a better career choice. Not wanting to become a nurse, I set an appointment to talk to the student counsellor to explore my options. However, the counsellor also thought that being a nurse would be the better choice. I inquired about the natural sciences programme, as I felt that it might have been a good choice that would allow me to make up my mind later, the reason being that successful completion of the natural sciences programme gave a pupil all the requirements necessary for all university programmes. Therefore, I felt this would buy me time to decide on what future path to take. However, the counsellor told me, "The natural sciences programme is extremely tough, and I am not sure it is the right choice for you." Being the person that I am, those words only fuelled my desire and further motivated me to pursuing the natural sciences programme.

Professional Career in Sweden

I applied and was accepted to the natural sciences programme at Fyrisskolan. Even though the negativity from the student counsellor had motivated me, I could not totally shake those words off, wondering if the programme was going to be too tough. However, as soon as I got through the first months, I knew that I was going to be fine. During the last semester in the programme, pupils were allowed to freely choose specific classes based on their interests. When some pupils saw this as an opportunity to reduce study load by not selecting classes, my schedule was filled with biology-oriented classes. I would borrow books on human pathogens and spend hours looking through them.

After completing high school, I decided to apply to the biomedical laboratory sciences bachelor programme at Örebro University. When I received the acceptance letter and before the start of the semester, my father and I made a trip to Örebro. I felt excited walking around the campus and finding my way to the department. When strolling around in the corridors, we were lucky enough to run into a student counsellor at the biomedical sciences programme. I asked if she had a moment to talk to me and was invited to her office. I inquired about student life and the content of the programme. About the programme, I was told, "It is a very intense programme and demands a lot from the students. So you have to be on top of things to succeed. Just so you know, some find it tough and drop off." Once again, I saw this as an opportunity to show myself what I was capable of. The semesters came and went, filled with interesting subjects including human anatomy, physiology, histology, and pathology. I learned about different diseases and different treatment schemes. I was able to find answers to some of the questions that had been circulating in my head from when I'd been growing up in Kenya. However, I also found out that many questions were yet to be answered. There was still a huge knowledge gap in the medical field, and this made me start wondering about ways to fill it. *How do people go about trying to answer these questions? Where do they begin? How are the studies done?* These were the new questions that started circulating in my head.

The last semester in the programme was spent working on a bachelor thesis, and I had looked forward to it, thinking that I might find answers to some of my questions. Eventually, it was time to pick a project for my thesis. Together with a classmate, we decided to contact a new research group leader who had just been recruited to the department. We set up an appointment and met the researcher who spoke so passionately about his research. He spoke about Vitamin A, cardiovascular diseases, inflammation, nuclear receptors, and transcription factors. It all sounded so complex, but the enthusiasm of the researcher was contagious. He handed us articles to read and asked us to give it a thought and then get back to him.

We were offered projects that were part of a larger project in the research group: investigation of the effects of vitamin A on inflammation. This project introduced me to the world of biomedical research, where I could dive into hypothesis-driven research. I enjoyed the challenge of trying to grasp the complex background of the hypothesis presented, and I spent a lot of time reading articles. We discussed the rationale behind study design, and I learned about setting up experiments, choosing analytical tools, and data analysis. I enjoyed discussing all of these aspects with my supervisor and other members of the laboratory. As soon as I got my data points, I could not wait to analyse and see what conclusions could be drawn.

I also learned that patience was an asset in the world of biomedical research. For instance, (i) some experiments take extremely long before data can be collected, (ii) to be able to set up a great hypothesis one has to spend a lot of time looking at the literature, and (iii) when setting up a new experiment, there is no guarantee that things will run smoothly. Just because something seemed plausible theoretically was not a guarantee that it would work in real life. I found research to be extremely rewarding as well to have your question, set up the experiments, and get your data points to interpret, then explain it all in writing. I presented and defended my thesis successfully and received my bachelor degree.

The previous two summers, I had held temporary positions as a laboratory assistant at university hospital laboratories in Uppsala and Örebro. After receiving my bachelor's degree, I worked at the laboratory in Örebro as a biomedical analyst. I spent my summer analysing patient samples for protein contents using different analytical approaches. The results were then relayed to the treating physician. I found myself thinking about the patients, their medications, and how the physician was going to use the test results in directing future treatment. This drove me to discuss different diseases and treatment options with the laboratory physicians. Once again, I found myself wanting to understand the mechanisms behind the disease and the drugs action. I realized that if I choose to keep on working in the laboratory with the diploma I had, I would continue doing routine analysis and probably not get the answers I was seeking. While it would have given me a stable income and stability in terms of employment, I could not help wonder whether it would make me happy. That was when I decided that I wanted to aim for a master's degree, as I felt that advancing may be the only way to feed my curiosity.

When I started looking into the possibilities for a master's project, I spoke to my bachelor-thesis advisor, but I was also approached by another research group leader who had been recruited to the department at the same time as my previous advisor. My bachelor-thesis advisor and I made a trip to Karolinska University Hospital in Stockholm where I was introduced to my advisor's former boss. He was an established researcher, both nationally and internationally, and a leading figure in the world of cardiovascular research. Studies from his laboratory had shaped this research field, and he later became a member of the Nobel Assembly of Karolinska Institute. As we walked through his laboratory, I heard about a lot of exciting projects that were being carried out in the laboratory. I got the opportunity to talk to him about my bachelor thesis, where I found myself feeling exhilarated talking about the experiments and the data I had collected. He then told me that I was welcomed to join his laboratory for a master thesis.

During my trip back to Örebro, it dawned on me that I had a tough decision to make. On one hand, I had a big research group that was well established internationally and on the leading edge producing paradigm-shifting research. The laboratory was big, with enormous resources, in an environment where the scientific critical mass was not confined to the research group, as there were many other research groups around. On the other hand, I had a smaller research group that was more isolated since there were not many biomedical research groups at the department on campus. However, I had integrated into that smaller research group, and I knew that I had great collegial support. I knew that I could easily knock on my advisor's door or call him whenever I had questions. I took the time to think carefully about the three options that had been put forth and then decided to join the laboratory where I had done my bachelor thesis.

I eagerly dove back into a world full of excitement, hard work, and frustration. I sensed that it was the only place that could nourish my curiosity. I studied the effects of retinol and its active derivatives on vascular smooth muscle cells. This time around, I learned the importance of working in a team and using the resources that come with it. The necessity of a critical mass for scientific and personal growth as a researcher, where research teams were working toward a common goal and constructive critiques in a supportive environment, lead to increased productivity. Moreover, I would often just knock on my bosses' door and discuss different aspects of the project, be it an analysis that was not going well or a new article related to the project. I was having so much fun, and I did not mind the late hours or weekends spent at the laboratory. After finishing my master thesis, my boss offered me a PhD thesis project, which I gladly accepted.

Now I had an office that I shared with another PhD student from another research group. Apart from the purely scientific part that I loved, I soon found out a lot of benefits that came with being a PhD student. You met other people with whom you shared the same interest. Even if you were not working on the same project or in the same research group, it increased the critical mass around you, which helped you become a better researcher. This also worked as a network of support and became a valuable asset for the future as the people you met would become your future colleagues. These people were not only PhD students but also other professors, senior researchers, postdoctoral fellows, and assistant professors. This created an interesting and great mixture which provided a great opportunity and environment for scientific growth. Moreover, in order to meet a larger critical mass, exchange ideas, and thereby increase the scientific creativity, research groups often went to conferences. Conferences provided a perfect chance to see where a specific area of research was heading, to get a new perspective, to make new contacts, and to meet prospective collaborators. While working on my PhD project, I travelled to different conferences in Europe and United States. I was always so amazed by the atmosphere at the conferences, where discussions about research never seemed to end, networks were forged, and new ideas were born. Moreover, as a very junior person in a coffee queue, I had the opportunity to converse with a senior frontier scientist.

There were many hours of frustration when experiments did not seem to work, articles were rejected, and grant applications did not make it through. However, the rewards always made those hours seem insignificant. The fact that I found myself working with nationally and internationally acknowledged physicians and scientists made me think, *It is great to be me!* Articles did get accepted, and I remember the excitement I felt the first time an article that I co-authored appeared in a medical research database, the thrill of typing "Pauline Ocaya" and having an article pop up. Knowing that I had co-authored an article that had been scrutinized by experts and had been found to qualify for publication felt amazing.

During my time at the department, I coached a number of students who came to the laboratory to work on their bachelor or master theses. I mentored them in experimental techniques, data collection, analysis, interpretation, and presentation. I also gave some classes in microbiology and medical statistics for students in the nursing programme and biomedical laboratory scientist programme. With each student I had and each lecture I gave, I was always thinking of ways to improve. *How could I make learning more enjoyable for the students?* I really liked the research and would try hard because I wanted the students to experience the beauty I saw. Consequently, I learned and improved my teaching skills. It made me realize that to be able to convey a message, one has to really know what one is talking about. I improved my technical skills and learned how to integrate better into a team. Together with the different activities that came from being part of a research team, I became better at networking and critical and analytical thinking, and I also had the great opportunity to travel and see new places and meet new people.

I felt that I had found a place that could nourish my curiosity. So, of course, I already knew my answer to the question asked by my boss towards the end of my PhD project: "What are your plans after your dissertation? Are you thinking of a postdoctoral training?"

"Yes, I would like to get a postdoctoral training. What are your thoughts on getting one in Sweden versus abroad?" I responded. He told me that training abroad was probably better. The conversation took place approximately a year and a half before I was due to defend my thesis and prior to a conference I was attending in the United States of America. Since I was heading to the United States, I spoke to my boss about the possibility of contacting research groups and going for interviews. We researched different research groups, and I contacted three groups to see whether they were interested in meeting with me. All three group leaders emailed me back, saying that they would like to meet. However, because of time restrictions and a business meeting that one of the group leaders had to attend in England, I was only able to make appointments to meet with two of the groups. So, in parallel with my conference, I took the opportunity to visit one laboratory at Miami University and another at the University of California, San Diego. There I met the lab members, discussed the research projects being conducted, and presented my doctoral project, and I was interviewed for a postdoctoral position.

Approximately four years after staring my PhD project, I defended my doctoral thesis at a dissertation with Professor William Blaner from Columbia University, New York, like my opponent. A few days prior to the dissertation, I researched my opponent, only to discover that when I was less than a year old, he had already published research articles in the field I was now in. So the thought of my work being scrutinized in front of an audience by someone who already was an expert long before I was born was quite nerve-wracking but at the same time somewhat exciting. Once our discussion started, I lost track of time and had to look at the clock when the professor said, "And now, to the last question…". It felt like we had been talking for half an hour, but in reality, two hours had passed. Somewhere along the way, I had forgotten about the audience and become totally focused on the discussion. This marked the end of my PhD project, and I moved to New York City (NYC) for a postdoctoral training at Weill Cornell Medical College, the reason being that the professor I had interviewed with in San Diego had relocated her laboratory to New York. Very excited to have the opportunity to live in NYC, I said goodbye to my family and friends and took off. All the paperwork, including contract, lease, and visa had been prepared and sent to me from New York prior to my departure. Based on what I had previously heard from people heading to the United States, I was expecting this part to be extremely complex, requiring a lot of time and energy. However, I was surprised by how swiftly and quickly it all went. I later found out that most research institutions in the United States were used to having researchers from all over the world coming to conduct research and, therefore, had routines in place making sure that everything ran smoothly and was finalized in a timely manner. Since all the paperwork was already in place, I had no problem getting into the country.

I arrived in NYC with one large suitcase, my laptop, and two addresses: one to the housing department where I would get the keys to my apartment, and one to the apartment. My postdoctoral advisor and lab mates took me out for dinner that same evening, and I started working the next morning. I felt that I was at the centre of an extremely strong biomedical research environment. For starters, three world-leading research institutes were located within a three block radius; Weill Cornell Medical College, Rockefeller University, and Memorial Sloan Kettering Cancer Centre. In Örebro, I had received a few couple of seminar announcements per week. Now I was suddenly unable to keep track of all the seminars being held per day at my department at Cornell. Planning experiments was also different. Previously, I had to take into account the time it took to receive reagents or to get a spot on an instrument and so forth. Now I could place an order and receive my reagents the day after. The department had many research groups, which increased the possibility of networking and creating collaborations, and it also meant a tremendous increase in the amount of resources.

(Pauline carrying out an experiment at her postdoctoral laboratory at Weill Cornell Medical College)

The main focus of the research being conducted in the new research group that I was now part of was embryonic vascular development – blood and lymphatic vasculature. This was an exciting research area that I knew little of but looked forward to learning more about. I immersed myself in it, and I enjoyed learning about stem cell biology, different mechanisms that regulate vascular development, and different techniques employed within the research area. Due to my training, I was now able to incorporate earlier knowledge and skills into my work. My boss gave my lab mates and me a lot of freedom by encouraging us to take our own initiatives and take part in leading the projects. Thus, I was actively part of all aspects of the project: setting up a hypothesis, designing the studies, carrying out the experiments, analysing the data, and getting the research ready for publication.

(Pauline at a Gordon Research Conference in Ventura County, California, presenting data from her research at Weill Cornell Medical College)

I had never been to New York prior to my postdoctoral training, and I did not think that Manhattan, a place I had never been to, would be the place I felt most at home. One of the reasons for this was that in contrast to my experience from Sweden, people did not seem that interested in where one came from. Often in Sweden, a few sentences in a conversation I would get questions like, "So where are you from?" or "Are you adopted? You speak Swedish really well," or "Were you born in Sweden? I can barely hear an accent." Having moved from place to place ever since I was little, I would, at first, be perplexed by the question, "Where are you from?" *What did they want to know? Was it my place of birth? Was it where my parents and siblings were living? Was it where I had lived longest, or was it which part of the city I was living in?* In Manhattan, one day during my less than ten minutes' walk from work, I encountered, at least, six different languages spoken along the way. *Living with such a great cultural variety probably makes people realize the insignificance of one's place of birth,* I thought.

Moving from Örebro to Manhattan meant changes in all kinds of ways. It was moving from a city with a population of approximately 130,000 to a borough with more than 1.6 million people. I was now living in this vibrant place, and I loved its pace. I could see a direct relation between the high pulse of the city and the pace at which people I met seemed to either be arriving in the city or just about to leave it. An acquaintance in New York once told me, "New York is one of the liveliest cities in the world, yet there is probably no other place in the world where one can feel so lonely." I could really see that in the high turnover I found amongst friends within academia. People I met through work and got close to would suddenly move to other places in the United States or back to their countries. At the same time, new postdoctoral fellows would be arriving. Regardless of this, I was able to develop close friendships that still remain intact five years later.

I enjoyed the cultural aspects of the city that span from cuisine to arts and music. Just heading downtown to Little Italy for pasta or to Chinatown for Chinese food or to Queens to have my favourite Thai cuisine. I would head to Harlem and go to the venue that once housed big names like Aretha Franklin, John Lennon and Yoko Ono, James Brown and Jimi Hendrix, just to name a few. Or I could go to an underground pub in Harlem to listen to blues musicians jamming. Or why not go to the East Village to listen to amateur musicians at Ludlow. I enjoyed just taking a walk to Central Park where each walk implied a new experience. Either you could bump into New York Philharmonic Orchestra playing at the park or see a game of soft ball or other performances held by world artists during summer. I loved the fact that I could leave work at 5.00 p.m. and, in less than two hours, be on the beach swimming in the Atlantic Ocean or within two hours be skiing down slopes in New Jersey or being amazed by the Niagara Falls. I took the opportunity to travel around the United States when possible. Seeing different places such as Las Vegas, the Grand Canyon, Los Angeles, San Francisco, Yellowstone National Park, and Washington, DC.

While in New York, I applied for and received funding from the Swedish Research Council for two-thirds of my postdoctoral training at Cornell. The funding also included research funds to be used in Sweden, for reincorporation into a Swedish research team. I came back to Sweden and joined a laboratory at Karolinska Institute. On two occasions, while still in NYC, I met a researcher who was in the process of starting her own research group at Karolinska Institute. The ongoing projects sounded extremely interesting, and also, the thought of being part of something new appealed to me. So after interviewing with two other research group leaders, one at the University of Oxford and the other in Lund in Sweden, I decided to join the laboratory at Karolinska Institute.

Years came and went, and my two-year contract at Karolinska quickly came to an end. During those two years at Karolinska Institute, I found myself becoming more and more fascinated by clinical research. Basic research was fun and exciting, yet the direct connection to patients that came with clinical research was extremely appealing too. I always found it very inspiring to listen to researchers presenting data demonstrating how their research had helped their patients. During my stay at Karolinska Institute, I attended a conference in Singapore, and data presented by a professor working on microbiota had a great effect on me. So, by the time my contract ended, I had decided that I wanted to become a medical doctor. I wanted to get back to the core of what had been driving me from the start – that feeling of helplessness I felt when facing my brother's illness when growing up, the curiosity that was present in me from early childhood, wanting to know more in order to help someone in need. I had wanted to understand the mechanisms behind diseases. Now with my scientific schooling, I hoped I would be able to take part in unveiling some of those mechanisms. Even though the road was still long and I did not yet know what I wanted to specialize in, I knew that a knowledge gap existed everywhere in medicine. This meant that there was a possibility for me to make things better for my future patients, regardless of what I chose to specialize in.

I enrolled in medical school, and I am currently beginning my fifth semester of medical programme at Umeå University. I had enjoyed teaching during my PhD project and had coached numerous students during my postdoctoral training at Cornell and at Karolinska Institute. Due to that interest, I contacted one of my professors at the department of Integrative Medical Biology, and I am currently teaching histology to small groups of students in the second and third semesters. Already from the beginning, I got involved in the Swedish Medical Students Association. Initially a member of the national board responsible for medical student's affairs at a national level, I am currently the president of the Umeå University section. During my period on the national board, I attended the Swedish Medical Association's annual council meeting. Those meetings are the highest decision-making body of the Swedish Medical Association, in which members of different professional associations and local associations are also represented. I could not help but wonder why I was the only black person in a room full of hundreds of medical doctors and some medical students. With the belief that one should be involved in the matters that concerns oneself, I remain active within the Swedish Medical Students Association. I am excited about the future and can barely wait to become a physician and combine medical research with clinical work.

(Pauline in a campaign at Umeå University to promote and make public the Students Association's new name)

Why Choose Higher Education?

Higher education allows you to acquire new skills and strengthen those you already possess. These skills can, later on, be used as tools that allow you to take control over your life. This applies to both professional and personal lives. For example, developing interpersonal skills will have a great impact on the kind of connections you forge with others. Professionally, it allows you to identify the course of action necessary to take in order to reach a specific goal even when in a team with individuals with whom you may not have much in common.

Your training makes you more equipped to take on challenges with the determination to complete them. With acquired analytical/problem-solving skills, you will be better prepared to handle pressure and to offer solutions to complex problems. This is possible because education provides the environment where you can challenge yourself, and by trying, practicing, and not giving up, you learn about yourself and what you are capable of. Knowing this will give you the confidence in a professional setting to take on new and more challenging projects because you will have learned that just because something looks impossible does not mean that it is.

Apart from problem-solving, communication, teamwork, and interpersonal abilities, higher education also gives you the opportunity to increase/acquire managerial, organizational competence, the ability to be responsible and increases your curiosity. All of these skills are those that employers around the world are looking for in an employee. Therefore, education will improve your chance of getting employed and getting to work with the job that you want to. Higher education gives you the opportunity to acquire deeper knowledge within your specific area of interest, making it easier to succeed both with studies and at work. It also means you become more specialized, which makes it possible to take on more specialized employments, and thereby boosting your career probability.

That said it does not rid of all obstacles out there. However, having an education prepares you better for overcoming them. Since higher education nourishes one's ability to think critically and analytically, it makes it easier to speak up when something does not feel right. It makes you pick up on things and makes you want to double-check. You look for facts instead of just taking someone's word for it or believing something the media, politicians, and so forth might be serving you. Most importantly, you will know where to look for the information, be it you are confronted by a doctorate, a lawyer, or an employee at the tax office. Tools you receive during your training will hopefully enable you to easily grasp different areas of expertise, which allows you to create your own understanding. This will lead to a healthier lifestyle, an increased ability to take place and time to educate your children and family and a greater interaction outside your area of expertise. You will be better equipped to take part in conversations in a qualified manner and hopefully be more open-minded.

Higher education also increases the opportunity of meeting different people within and outside your field of interest and to network with future colleagues, and it creates the chance to meet close friends. Working together with people who are driven, but also meeting people seeing things from different point of view, leads to personal growth and less close-mindedness. It may also forge bounds that may last forever. I met my closest friend ten years ago when working on my PhD project. Acquiring good interpersonal skills may allow for connections that increase chances for employment, thereby lessening the risk of eventually remaining unemployed for long periods.

You know what your qualification is worth and so do employers. Knowing your worth increases your confidence, allowing you to stand up for yourself in a different way that hopefully leads to increased equality, both at work and at home. Altogether, higher education makes your grow, opens roads and increases the likelihood of being in charge of one's life.

Experiences and Recommendations to Young People of African Background

One of my driving forces has been aiming to defy those who, for whatever reason, thought I was not good enough. I am extremely stubborn. I aim high, and I will push myself. And at the same time, I enjoy proving people wrong. So one of the ways I got motivated to keep on moving forward was when someone said, "Do you really think you can do that? It is extremely difficult, and I doubt you will succeed." On that note, do not allow anyone to make you doubt yourself based on what they think "someone like you" is or is not be capable of.

When getting advice, try to analyse what it is based on. Is it based on a correct assessment of your capacities? People may think that they mean well but unknowingly, or even worse, knowingly, are giving you advice based on a prejudgement. So take some time and reflect on what is being put in front of you. Look at it from different angles. If you cannot identify where the advice came from, talk to someone you trust on that specific subject. Be it about education or job, choose accordingly. If possible, identify someone you look up to and make him or her your mentor. Approach that person when in doubt. But remember that he or she is also a human being and may have clouded judgement.

Sounding like my father, I would say to aim for something that gives you a degree or certificate that you can pull out and say, "This is what I have done, so what I can do for you and your cooperation is this and that." You may not always have your goals clear, but start somewhere. Anywhere is better than standing still; not moving forward. Pushing forward increases the possibility of identifying what it is that you really are excited about.

Aim as high as you can; that is the only way to challenge yourself and grow. The road will probably be tough, and you will end up doubting yourself more than once. However, keep in mind that at times, this doubt may not be due to your inability. You may feel you have to work much harder than those around you to prove your worth. With your qualifications and knowing those around you, you will be able to identify the situations that you should not be taking personally. Because, as we know, colour does matter. So when you see that whatever is happening to you seems to be purely of discriminatory nature, open your case containing all the skills you possess and identify the next course of action. Lastly, do your best to identify opportunities and grab them. Be proactive!

Bringing It All Together

By illustrating the stories of three women of African descent, all with very diverse socio-economic backgrounds, this book shows that attaining higher education matters, and education can be used as a tool to overcome some obstacles in one's life. Higher education is a tool that can contribute towards living a more fulfilling life, and the spillover effects can influence others positively, particularly children. There is no doubt that high education is also contributing to an emerging African-Swedish middle class. As evidenced by Pauline's story, curiosity has been a huge driving force for her generation and more so for the ones coming behind her. In the case of Sarah's story, her determination not to let circumstances stop her from achieving her goals is a great inspiration to many others. Linley's story, demonstrates that sheer determination and memories of how girls could not get opportunities for higher education as the boys back in Malawi drove her to seek higher education. Linley propelled by her father, while Sarah was encouraged by her grandmother. All three women were resolute about tapping into the opportunities, and the environment in Sweden provided a haven for them to pursue higher education.

When the three of us arrived in Sweden, our education enabled us to quickly get integrated into the society. It was not without challenges, but with sheer relentless determination, we made our dreams become realities. Even after more than two decades, there is no doubt that it is more and more about the survival of the fittest immigrants, regardless of their ethnicity. Those who are innovative and willing to go that extra mile to master the Swedish language as well as to equip themselves with higher education and skills are most likely to achieve their professional dreams. What got us here today will not get us there tomorrow. We have to keep reinventing and affirming each other, especially our younger generation of African Swedes. Statistically, there are fewer students enrolled in universities with one or both parents of African-Swedish decent. So the question is: where do people of African-Swedish descent end up? What is it that influences their choices or possibilities for undertaking higher education studies all the way to a PhD level?

Regardless of where you find yourself today do not allow circumstances to be a hindrance to reaching your full potential. The stories of the three women in this book should motivate, encourage, or affirm that making the choice to study for a long time is a meaningful cause. No matter what you choose to do thereafter, an education can never be stripped away from you. Higher education will always be beneficial to you and a means to reach your life goals at any point in life and in any society.

Each and every human being is unique, and every personal story is unique. What is your story?